PRAISE FOR
THE DIGITAL EXPERIENCE COMPANY

"The world has gone remote, and very often the only way to interact with customers is through a digital channel. Alfonso's book focuses on a topic many leaders have still not fully grasped today: to stay competitive in the digital economy you need to deliver a great digital experience and focus on the customer. The book helps you understand why it's so important to focus on product design, customer happiness, and user research. I highly recommend this book to anyone looking to upgrade their digital footprint."

—Eric Yuan, CEO and founder, Zoom

"In the SaaS (software as a service) digital economy we live in, if the end user doesn't have a great experience, they will inevitably churn. It's therefore imperative that, in order to be successful in the digital marketplace, companies invest in delivering a great product experience to drive retention and growth. Alfonso understands what it takes to make great digital product experiences happen."

—Nick Mehta, CEO, Gainsight

"All companies are software driven (at least partly), many customer interactions are digital, and brand is experience. Any of these three is enough to care about user experience, but the combo means that UX is destiny. This book explains all this. More importantly, it explains what to do about it. Read and prosper—or ignore and die."

—Jakob Nielsen, PhD, user advocate and principal, Nielsen Norman Group

"At a time when companies obsess over big data and agile delivery, Alfonso de la Nuez delivers a critical message: how to interweave complementary insights about the digital experience of the customer into modern business practices at scale."

—Christian Rohrer, PhD, senior director of design, McAfee

"The new reality is that every business is a digital experience company. Alfonso has shown the clear connection between user experience (UX) and customer experience (CX) along with practical guidance on how to get started on a necessary transformation to get ahead of your competition."

—Webb Stevens, board member, BPD Zenith

"In the era of digital transformation and the experience economy, this book takes a deep dive into why, what, and how individuals and organizations can deliver consumer-grade experiences on top of enterprise-grade back end to make user experience a competitive advantage. It explains, with examples, the not-so-secret sauce of 'test early and often' and 'fail fast' without getting lost in data. A must read!"

—Kuldeep Kelkar, senior vice president, User Experience Research, UserZoom; former director, User Experience and Design, PayPal

digital

experience

ALFONSO DE LA NUEZ

—— THE ——

digital experience

—— COMPANY ——

WINNING IN THE DIGITAL ECONOMY
WITH EXPERIENCE INSIGHTS

ForbesBooks

Published by ForbesBooks, Charleston, South Carolina.
Member of Advantage Media Group.

ForbesBooks is a registered trademark, and the ForbesBooks colophon is a trademark of Forbes Media, LLC.

Printed in the United States of America.

10 9 8 7 6 5 4 3 2 1

ISBN: 978-1-946633-99-6
LCCN: 2021922055

This custom publication is intended to provide accurate information and the opinions of the author in regard to the subject matter covered. It is sold with the understanding that the publisher, Advantage|ForbesBooks, is not engaged in rendering legal, financial, or professional services of any kind. If legal advice or other expert assistance is required, the reader is advised to seek the services of a competent professional.

Advantage Media Group is proud to be a part of the Tree Neutral® program. Tree Neutral offsets the number of trees consumed in the production and printing of this book by taking proactive steps such as planting trees in direct proportion to the number of trees used to print books. To learn more about Tree Neutral, please visit **www.treeneutral.com**.

Since 1917, Forbes has remained steadfast in its mission to serve as the defining voice of entrepreneurial capitalism. ForbesBooks, launched in 2016 through a partnership with Advantage Media Group, furthers that aim by helping business and thought leaders bring their stories, passion, and knowledge to the forefront in custom books. Opinions expressed by ForbesBooks authors are their own. To be considered for publication, please visit **www.forbesbooks.com**.

CONTENTS

Why I Had to Write This Book

*Assists is what Earvin is all about. That's what
my whole life has been, assisting others.*
—EARVIN "MAGIC" JOHNSON

I've had the good fortune to meet former Los Angeles Lakers basketball star Earvin "Magic" Johnson twice in my life—a dream come true for a basketball lover from Spain—and those two meetings bracketed my realization of the American Dream. That realization includes founding and becoming the CEO of a more than $100 million company called UserZoom. How I got from a relatively modest household in Madrid, Spain, to running a successful international company in Silicon Valley is quite a story—and that story ties in with why I want to help other businesspeople realize their dreams for their companies in a digital age that offers great opportunities but also a myriad of pitfalls.

I loved basketball when I was growing up and worked hard to get good at it—to the point where, at age fifteen, I was recruited by the Real Madrid club to a minor league squad. They would recruit talented kids early and groom them. I really wanted to go professional, and this was the first step. But then my parents got this idea that I should go to the US for a year as a foreign exchange student. I didn't want to stop playing basketball for the Real Madrid feeder team, but Mom convinced me to go for my junior year. However, I insisted that they find me a high school that had a basketball program, so I could keep playing and improving my skills, and I also asked that the school be in California, because I was a huge Lakers—and especially Magic Johnson—fan. They found a school in Ramona, near San Diego, and off I went.

It was tough at first, because I did not speak the language well, and in 1989 there was no Internet, no mobile phones (so no cheap way to call Europe), no easy way to communicate with folks back home. It was mostly letters, written on plain white paper: the good old-fashioned way. So I had a difficult time for six months, just trying to adjust. Luckily, the school had a wonderful basketball program led by coach Al Schaffer (with whom I am still very close and consider family). I thought I was going to be warming the bench and just trying to learn from the talented American players, but I ended up being the high scorer on the team and holding the high school record in assists. I also started speaking English better. So the second half of the year, things got much better.

For my birthday, in February, Coach Schaffer took me to the Forum for a Lakers game. It was a dream come true to watch Magic Johnson and all the other Lakers in action live for the first time! Afterward, Coach—who was from Michigan, like Magic Johnson—took me down to the entrance to the hallway that led to the locker rooms and told the guards that we had to see "Buck," which was Magic's nickname back in Michigan. He made it sound like he was Magic's friend. They refused us admission at first, but Coach Schaffer persisted—he is a pretty determined guy—and eventually they let us in!

So, there I was, a sixteen-year-old Spaniard, in the hallway with my Lakers hat on and my autograph picture in my hand, watching the other Lakers—James Worthy, Michael Cooper, Mychal Thompson (Klay Thompson's dad) … all of them!—leaving the Forum. We waited there for two hours after the game. It was past midnight, and we still had to drive for two hours to get back to Ramona. So I really did not think the meeting was going to happen.

But then, lo and behold, Magic emerged. He had been told that a high school coach from Michigan was out there and wanted to say hello. He was wearing jeans and a white sweater—I will never forget that image. He came up to us and said hello, and Coach said, "Alfonso here is one of my players. He chose to wear number thirty-two, just like you, because you are his hero. He's here all the way from Spain!"

Magic gave me a high five and was super kind, with his big, warm smile. I told him, "I play just like you." And he laughed like crazy and said, "Oh my God, is that right? Is that right, now?" And it was true. While I was a pretty good shooter, like him I loved the art of passing and dishing out assists to make others around me

better, to help my teammates succeed. Magic inspired me then, and he still inspires me now.

In an interview with the *Wall Street Journal*, another Lakers star, Kobe Bryant, said that he enjoyed helping others succeed too. "The most important thing I enjoy now is helping others be successful. I enjoy doing that much more; that's something that lasts forever. That's my definition of true success." I couldn't have put it better myself.

To this day, I believe as a manager that true success means "assisting" and enabling others—empowering your team to grow, develop, and succeed. There's nothing more powerful than a team with the same mission and vision pursuing success—and I got that philosophy from watching Magic Johnson, and then Kobe Bryant, dishing assists and making all the players around him better.

After spending my junior year in high school in California and being away from my family and friends for a year, you'd figure I'd have wanted to go back and stay in beautiful Madrid. But destiny had other plans for me. I ended up staying in Ramona for my senior year and winning a basketball scholarship to San Jose State University, right in the heart of Silicon Valley. During the years I was coming of age there, from 1991 to 1996, the commercial Internet was coming of age too—and I was in the middle of it. The World Wide Web was born in the early 1990s; AOL and the Mosaic web browser came along in 1993; full-text web search engines appeared in 1994; and in 1996 AOL established the monthly (instead of hourly) pricing model that is still used by most SaaS companies. From then on, it was no-holds-barred commercial development for the Internet.

As a young man from Spain studying international business administration, I was fascinated by the international commercial possibilities of this new medium. I explored it as much as possible in those early days and imagined what it could do for users and customers. I was passionate about it. So much so that when I returned to Spain with my degree (pro basketball did not work out for me), I took a job as a project manager in charge of building the first versions of the websites for many Spanish companies. I also met my wife, a web designer, at that company!

What I came to realize during this role was that websites, as they were being approached then, were about what the engineers, the designers, and the company executives wanted—and very little about what the actual *end user* wanted. No attempt was made to find out how well the website would serve the people who were actually going to *use* it! This wonderful new technology was actually not easy to use at all! This ultimately led me to establish, with two cofounders, a usability testing company called Xperience Consulting. We didn't offer any website design or development services; we just did usability testing for business websites—but that was a new and desperately needed service at the time (2001, right before the World Trade Center terrorist attack, right after the famous dot-com bubble market crash).

The business did very well, and I was enjoying a good life in my hometown, Madrid. The problem was that this service was people intensive when done in person, which made it very costly and hard to scale. So a few years later, we designed a software product we called UserZoom to automate the process and scale user experience (UX) research. But when we looked at the market in Spain and Europe, we realized it was too sophisticated for most companies there at the time. However, we thought it would be appealing to UX-sensitive technology companies in Silicon Valley and across the US—companies like eBay, Google Yahoo, PayPal, IBM, and so on: companies that really cared about the quality of their users' experience.

Because of my seven years living in California as a student, my knowledge of the US culture, and my fluency in English, we decided that I would move back to the US to market UserZoom. We quickly got several companies interested, including eBay and Google, and that was the beginning of the UserZoom company that has become highly successful.

Fast-forward to today, where the nature and needs of companies are completely different because of the digital revolution—it's almost like another galaxy! Building a great website or app is a multimillion-dollar project that generates billions of dollars in revenue, and many more companies are *purely* digital experience companies.

And that is why I had to write this book. There is so much more at stake now than there was fourteen years ago, when UserZoom was founded. Consumers, in almost all situations, interact with brands through a digital channel. Companies, both start-ups and large corporations in both B2C (business to consumer) and B2B (business to business), can rise to great heights and enjoy tremendous success for many years or fail very quickly and dramatically, depending on the quality of the digital experience they provide for their customers and potential customers. Now more than ever, you need to understand the tremendous value of great user experience (UX) design, as well as UX research, and you need to understand why they are impactful to the business and how to do it right.

Now, there are plenty of great books focused on design and research practices and methodologies, with plenty of "how-to" knowledge. While this book does address some of this as well (see chapters 5 and 6), it is mainly targeted at business leaders, such as C-level executives (CEOs, CPOs, CIOs, and CTOs), product leaders, heads of digital or e-commerce, as well as capital investors (venture capitalists or private equity funds), with a focus on the value of great design and its impact (ROI) on digital business success. That is what *The Digital Experience Company* will teach you.

This book will show you why and how every company must now see user experience as its new business strategy, as well as the common challenges related to it; how to design and develop a great digital experience; how to understand the users' goals and how they differ from company goals; how to figure out how user research metrics differ from (but also influence) business KPIs; and how to measure the return on your investment in user research.

You *can* succeed in the digital age—the opportunities are astounding—and I'd like to help you achieve that success. Because, like my hero Magic Johnson, I get my satisfaction from helping others achieve their full potential.

CHAPTER 1

Why Every Company Is a Digital Experience Company

In short, software is eating the world.
—MARC ANDREESEN

What Marc Andreesen, the founder of Netscape and now a venture capitalist at Andreessen Horowitz, meant to say in the quote above from back in 2011—in a brief, pithy way—is that more and more businesses and industries are being run on software and delivered as online services, and more and more consumers are interacting with companies' brands through digital channels and digital products. Fast-forward to today: more often than not the digital experience is the *only* experience consumers will have of your brand—or at least a much more significant part of it than the live experience. In fact, according to McKinsey & Company research, over 60 percent of all customer interactions and product or service offerings in North America are now digital—with that percentage only expected to grow.[1]

The COVID-19 crisis has accelerated the digitization of customer interactions by several years.

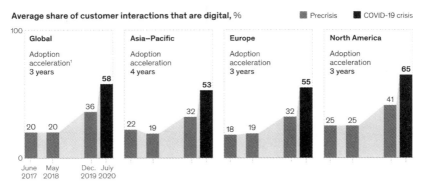

Average share of customer interactions that are digital, %

'Years ahead of the average rate of adoption from 2017 to 2019.

McKinsey
& Company

During the dot-com bubble years and even through the following decade, this kind of interaction with consumers was more often limited to purely digital companies, so-called dot-coms, whose reason for being was to foster digital interactions. But now, consumers don't have to be in a digital space anymore to interact digitally. Virtually every kind of company—even traditionally brick-and-mortar companies such as retailers, banks, delivery companies, insurance companies, healthcare providers, and so on—are interacting regularly with their customers digitally.

And, of course, the 2020 COVID-19 lockdowns accelerated this trend dramatically. Satya Nadella, Microsoft CEO, recently said that "we've seen two years of digital transformation in two months."

---

1   "How COVID-19 has pushed companies over the technology tipping point—and transformed business forever," McKinsey, accessed October 18, 2021, https://www.mckinsey.com/business-functions/strategy-and-corporate-finance/our-insights/how-covid-19-has-pushed-companies-over-the-technology-tipping-point-and-transformed-business-forever.

Companies were not only forced to interact with their customers digitally, and vice versa, but they also discovered efficiencies and economies of scale through digital interaction, and so did their customers.

What this means for your organization is that, in order to survive and thrive, you *must* recognize that, now and forever, *all companies are essentially digital companies.* And not just digital companies, but digital *experience* companies. The sooner you understand this and create a strategy that takes advantage of it, the more likely you are to be successful.

What is the difference between a digital company and a digital *experience* company?

Up until recently, being digital meant you had the necessary IT (information technology) infrastructure (the commonly called "back-end systems") to support your digital property, such as a website for e-commerce. Being digital was all about having great technology. But now, the technology needed to be a digital company is available off the shelf, with the likes of AWS (Amazon Web Services), Stripe, etc. This means more and more companies and competitors *can* actually create a digital experience. But what makes it good and differentiates them from the rest? It's not the technology itself but how good the experience is with that technology. And that is felt in the hearts and minds of the end user.

The business world has gone from just offering some kind of interaction with products via technology to actually offering a truly holistic *digital experience.* It's not just about people interacting with

> **In order to survive and thrive, you *must* recognize that, now and forever, *all companies are essentially digital companies.***

some back-end technology—the consumer doesn't see any of that! It's about the quality of the experience your users and customers have interacting with your product and with your brand—can they do what they want to do easily, and do they have a great experience doing it?

Being a digital experience company, therefore, means it's critical to have a killer UI (user interface) and UX (user experience)—and that is not just about back-end technology. How usable and pleasing the user's interaction with that technology is depends on having a great *front-end design*, a presentation of your products that provides a great experience for users, that endears them to your brand, that enhances ease of use and convenience above all else, and that keeps them coming back for more. If you don't give them this, they will eventually leave if they can—often immediately—and evidence shows that they aren't likely to come back! As an example, an Accenture report from 2017 shows 61 percent of consumers switched business from one brand to another in the past year.[2] A great front end isn't a bonus anymore; it's just the starting point—you *must* provide it! People aren't impressed just by background technology anymore (in fact they don't care at all about that); they want a UX that lets them accomplish what they need to accomplish simply and pleasantly. This is a fact for both B2C and B2B brands, and even in the enterprise market today. In order to be a digital *experience* company, you need to have strong, secure, enterprise-grade back-end technology *and* a consumer-grade front-end user experience.

The other way that software is "eating the world" is by keeping people digitally connected all the time and anywhere—at home, in

---

2   Robert Wollan et al, "Seeing Beyond the Loyalty Illusion: It's Time You Invest More Wisely," Accenture Strategy, accessed October 18, 2021, https://www.accenture. com/t00010101T000000__w__/pl-pl/_acnmedia/Accenture/Conversion-Assets/ DotCom/Documents/Global/PDF/Strategy_8/Accenture-Strategy-GCPR-Customer-Loyalty_PoV.pdf.

their cars, walking down the street, etc. The so-called cloud computing and the ubiquitous portable access to a computing device (smartphones, tablets, and laptops), and their wireless connection to the Internet, make this possible. It is a rare moment when people are *not* connected to the Internet in one way or another. This continuous connection has enabled companies to sell many kinds of applications using the software-as-a-service (SaaS) model—a subscription model that has consumers interacting with a company's product(s) or website through a browser on demand and for a specific period of time, instead of downloading the application. This makes distribution easy and economical for the providers of SaaS.

A good example of this is the online version of Microsoft Word, which I used with my editor while working on this book. In the past, I'd have had to buy a CD-ROM in a box from a store, insert it in my computer, download the entire program onto my computer's hard drive, and then use it. When it had to be updated, I'd have to download the upgrade from the Internet. Now I buy a subscription on Office.com, access Word from the cloud, and the version of the file is continually and automatically updated by Microsoft's cloud service. And if I decide I'm not happy with Word, I can end my subscription and subscribe to another word processing app.

When people bought an application and physically loaded it to their computers (with a CD ROM, for example), it was there for a long time, and there was little interaction between company and consumer. But with the SaaS model, also called "access economy," versus "ownership economy," consumers can access your products or services *from any device at any time, so they are continually interacting with your brand and a newly revised version of your product.* This is a huge game changer. When people downloaded a product to their computer, they tended to stick with it, to accept the bad with the good. But now, because of this new paradigm, your product's experience, including its presentation, must be superior. This is because if your UX doesn't give consumers what they want or frustrates them, they will simply cancel the subscription and find someone who provides a UX that is more appealing. In Microsoft's case, for instance, users could move to competitors such as Google Docs or Apple Pages, given how relatively easy and inexpensive it is to switch products.

So while SaaS has all kinds of benefits for providers—easy sale, distribution, and upgrading, among many others—the business model is fundamentally different. It will take a significant investment and time to build a product that works well in this environment and then to recoup the sizeable investment that building it will require. Subscriptions bring in revenue in a much more fragmented way and over a longer period of time, so you'll have to work even harder to retain current customers and win new ones. You also need to expand your penetration of individual companies and markets by getting wider use within organizations that adopt your product.

All of this is dependent on creating a great UX backed up with a great overall customer experience (CX). That will enable you to win customers, retain customers, expand the number of users within existing customers, and expand adoption, usage, and awareness of your product's value and ease of use through the press, social media, and word-of-mouth recommendations. In 2007, the iPhone really put the importance of UX on the map. Apple created a UX that was so far superior to anything else out there that it changed the world. Then sites like Yelp, Twitter, Facebook, and many other social media and consumer review platforms gave consumers a kind of power they'd never had before to do things they wanted to do easily and quickly. Providing a great UX and giving users power through their apps have become increasingly important over time and will be increasingly important far into the future—and any company that doesn't realize this will pay the price.

Being Digital Means Being Mega Customer Centric and Data Driven

I'm a big fan of both Amazon's UX and CX—and not only because they're a UserZoom customer. Amazon understands that *being a digital experience company means that you are a true customer-centric company*! While not necessarily the easiest to use or most visually appealing, the Amazon website works very effectively, gives you the information you need, when you need it, and guides you to where you need to go—and then it delivers what you want efficiently and effectively. Any issues, returns, and refunds are as easy as one-two-three.

If you're used to using Amazon, dealing with another retailer's site can be eye opening. My wife and I are huge fans of a certain clothing company, and we've often ordered their products via Amazon, but I decided to go to their website and order directly from them in order to support the company during the COVID-19 crisis. What I experienced as I used their website for the first time was not that positive. First of all, their product-search filtering mechanism wasn't all that good—it wasn't easy to narrow down the clothes I was searching for. When I finally found what I wanted, there were no reviews of it—no fitting guide saying whether it ran small or large, if the material was comfortable, and so on—meaning I was, in a way, buying half-blind. But I liked what I saw, so I went ahead and purchased several items anyway.

> **Being a digital experience company means that you are a true customer-centric company!**

Two days after I made the purchase, I got an email saying that one of the items of clothing I had ordered was out of stock—two days! Supply and availability information like this should obviously be integrated and updated real time in the user interface (UI) so that a customer knows instantly—like they do on Amazon—if a product is in stock or not. Then the rest of my order didn't arrive, and I couldn't find any information on the website about where it was and what was happening to it. But they did link me to the USPS site, which said it had been delivered—which it had not. I called customer support and asked what they would do about this, but they said that if I hadn't gotten the package, I had to talk to the post office about it *myself.* This is not good customer service nor a good customer experience, and it really put me off the brand. This is something they should have been willing to investigate *for* me.

This and the other shortcomings of this clothing company's UX and CX sent me scurrying back to Amazon, where I know instantly whether I'm going to be able to get something, what it's like, and when I'm getting it—which can be overnight or even the same day with some products. And with Amazon, I know I can conveniently return items by slapping on a label Amazon provides. This is why Amazon is such an astoundingly successful digital experience company. They have the UX-CX combination down pat.

The clothing retailer I dealt with needs to learn how to do this, how to truly be a digital experience company, in order to compete with Amazon or to simply attract first-time buyers and retain customers. *Inside Design* says that 88 percent of online consumers who have a bad experience on a website are less likely to return![3] This retailer has to connect its online ordering system to its inventory system; they have

---

3   Jozef Toth, "13 Impressive Statistics on User Experience," *Inside Design*, November 24, 2015, https://www.invisionapp.com/inside-design/statistics-on-user-experience/.

to build an e-commerce engine; they have to design a better UX at the front end that makes shopping more convenient and helpful for their users before they become customers. And in order to win loyal customers, they need to figure out how to create a good postpurchase CX that provides follow-through with those customers. This is all part of being a customer-centric company. You must deeply understand the customer and make their interactions as easy and convenient as possible for them.

IKEA is a traditionally brick-and-mortar company that has come around to realizing the importance of being a digital experience company. This is a particularly strong example, because IKEA was *so much* a brick-and-mortar company that they put care into the design of the consumer experience in their stores! Over the past couple of years, however, they've gone digital big time, hiring the experienced professionals (including dozens of UX designers and researchers) they need to translate their international brand to an online setting and make it effective in that setting. Moreover, in 2017 IKEA acquired TaskRabbit, the very popular on-demand platform for hiring people to do everything from build furniture to stand in line for you at the Apple Store to make consumers' everyday life at home easier by connecting them with flexible and affordable ways to get their to-dos done.

Swedish multinational clothing retailer H&M is another brick-and-mortar retailer that has upped their digital experience game in the evolving economy. Adding UX research to their digital experience product development process (which we will discuss in the following chapters of the book) allowed them to reduce time to checkout by 84 percent, resulting in a 4 percent increase in online checkout conversions. Proof that a great experience can directly impact the bottom line!

This is what virtually all traditionally brick-and-mortar companies need to do. The COVID-19 lockdowns made it a necessity temporarily, but that crisis only hastened a process that was already well on its way before the crisis. The younger generation is digitally focused to a degree that is far beyond their elders, and they are the customers of the future—and actually, they're pretty active digital consumers already!

The Business Case for Great UX and CX

Before we get into the business case for having a great digital UX and overall CX, let's get some basic definitions for our terms. I'll include UI, because although UI is ultimately part of UX, the term is used so commonly that it should be defined. I've drawn these basic definitions from Wikipedia:

- UI, as part of UX, is "the space where interactions between humans and machines occur. The goal of this interaction is to allow effective operation and control of the machine from the human end, whilst the machine simultaneously feeds back information that aids the operators' decision-making process.... Generally, the goal of user interface design is to produce a user interface which makes it easy, efficient, and enjoyable (user friendly) to operate a machine in the way which produces the desired result (i.e., maximum usability)."

- UX is "a person's emotions and attitudes about using a particular product, system, or service. It includes the practical, experiential, affective, meaningful, and valuable aspects of human-computer interaction and product ownership. Additionally, it includes a person's perceptions of system aspects such as utility, ease of use, and efficiency."

- CX is "the product of an interaction between an organization and a customer over the duration of their relationship. This interaction is made up of three parts: the customer journey, the brand touchpoints the customer interacts with, and the environments the customer experiences (including digital environment) during their experience."

- Service design, according to Wikipedia, is the activity of planning and arranging people, infrastructure, communication, and material components of a service in order to improve its quality, and the interaction between the service provider and its users.

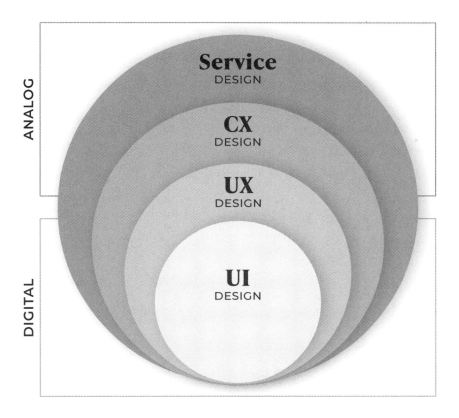

If all of these elements are combined and done well, across any part of the customer journey, they then provide the ultimate experience for people who interact with your company. And there is a tremendous return on investment for companies that deliver this kind of experience.

I'll go over a real-life example of how UX and CX are related in the upcoming section called "Great UX + Great CX = Business Success."

The COVID-19 pandemic of 2020 accelerated the increasing shift of consumers to online channels, pushing digital adoption to new levels worldwide. According to research from McKinsey & Company, as of July 2020, 58 percent of customer interactions were digital (up from 36 percent in December 2019)—a three-year acceleration from the 2017 to 2019 period. Furthermore, 55 percent of the products or services being offered by businesses were partially or fully digitized—a massive seven-year acceleration, up from 35 percent in December 2019.[4] With the majority of interactions now taking place in the digital realm, and companies shifting their offering portfolios toward digital, the importance of understanding, measuring, and improving digital experience— and with it the level of risk and capital at stake—has become paramount for businesses hoping to survive and thrive in the new economy.

---

4   "How COVID-19 has pushed companies over the technology tipping point—and transformed business forever," McKinsey, accessed October 18, 2021, https://www. mckinsey.com/business-functions/strategy-and-corporate-finance/our-insights/ how-covid-19-has-pushed-companies-over-the-technology-tipping-point-and-transformed-business-forever.

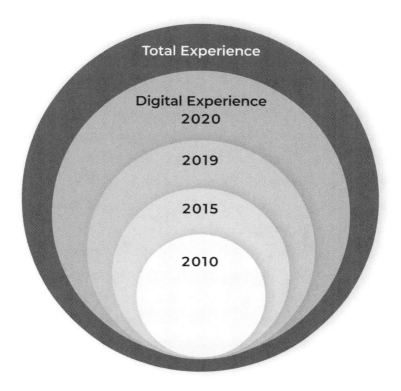

If you have any doubt that delivering a great UX and CX is imperative to business success, I have some news for you: in 2019, SAP, one of the largest corporations in the world, bought Qualtrics, the leading experience management platform, for a whopping $8 billion! Clearly SAP considers customer experience essential to the future of businesses.

And SAP is not alone in recognizing the value of CX. In a report on the relationship between UX and CX, Jane-Anne Mennella, senior director analyst at Gartner, wrote, "User experience is critical to ensuring a successful customer experience. But CX leaders face confusion and lack of integration between these two disciplines, undermining the power of both."[5]

---

5   Jane-Anne Mennella, *Integrate User Experience into Your Customer Experience to Improve Outcomes*, Gartner Research, April 14, 2020.

David Truog, VP of research at Forrester Research, in a report called "Demystifying the Language of CX and UX," says, "Most companies now understand that the quality of customer experiences drives business results. But your colleagues who misunderstand key cX/uX concepts risk botching strategic decisions."[6]

According to a Forrester report on the business impact of good UX design in customer interfaces, studies from McKinsey & Company, the Design Management Institute, and the UK Design Council confirm that companies that focus on good UX design get benefits such as greater customer loyalty, increased revenue, a higher market valuation, and better-performing stock.[7] And this is true for companies from large public corporations to start-ups. Here are a few of the examples that the report provides:

- Business intelligence company (with NTT DATA) improved the ease of use of their shopping cart and thereby improved its conversion rate 77 percent (320 percent among repeat users).

- U.S. Bank (with Genpact) corrected the design of the tool that helped issuers and investors track collateralized loan obligations (CLOs) and gained a 40 percent increase in their market share as a CLO trustee over the first year.

- PayPal removed jargon and legal terminology from their international checkout to make it clearer and easier to use and achieved a significant increase in conversion and revenue.

6   David Truog, "Demystifying the Language of CX and UX," Forrester, October 2, 2018, https://www.forrester.com/report/Demystifying-The-Language-Of-CX-And-UX/RES144655.

7   Benedict Sheppard et al., "The Business Value of Design," McKinsey & Company, October 25, 2018, https://www.mckinsey.com/business-functions/mckinsey-design/our-insights/the-business-value-of-design.

And another example, from the InVision online article "13 Impressive Statistics on User Experience," is that ESPN.com revenues jumped 35 percent after they listened to their community and incorporated that community's suggestions into their homepage redesign.[8]

Why does paying attention to UX help companies succeed? For one thing, many products and services are becoming commoditized in the digital world, because consumers have access to so many more choices via the Internet than they had when all interactions were live. Take banking, for example. The same banking products and services are available from an endless number of providers.

Companies that focus on good UX design get benefits such as greater customer loyalty, increased revenue, a higher market valuation, and better-performing stock.

So how does a bank differentiate itself? How does it offer something that is different? Is it through offering a better loan rate or higher interest on accounts?

Yes, certainly. But that's not enough anymore. Bank choices have traditionally been impacted largely by two factors: (1) physical presence and convenience of a branch to go into, and (2) parental influence (kids usually stick with the bank their parents set them up with when they are minors). Today, banks must deliver great digital experiences, because so much of banking is now digital, and banks cannot rely on factors (1) and (2) to grow their businesses in the future. Consumers today choose a bank not only for rational reasons, such as getting better rates, but also because that bank provides a great

---

8   Jozef Toth, "13 Impressive Statistics on User Experience," InVision, accessed October 18, 2021, https://www.invisionapp.com/inside-design/statistics-on-user-experience/.

website and/or app that is convenient to use and therefore makes their life easier. So banks, like many other businesses, are becoming digital experience companies, and they're competing on the quality of the experience they provide their customers. They're delivering not only their services but also their *brand* through their digital channels.

In order to succeed in our increasingly digital world, your website or app *must* produce a great experience for users and potential customers. Just having a digital *presence* isn't enough. If you want to compete in the marketplace today, if you want to have strong positioning—if you really want to "eat" the market you're in—then you need to provide a great experience through your digital channels.

The Path to Great UI and UX

I've established how important it is in our digital world to have a killer UX, so the next question is, How do you get there?

First of all, it's not easy to build a high-quality digital experience—one that meets both new users' and returning customers' expectations. Even being in the UX market, we at UserZoom, a feature-rich, fairly complex enterprise software research application, have taken a while to improve our own product UX. People sometimes complain about how many businesses still have imperfect digital products with poor usability, but I'm sympathetic to many of these businesses. At the same time, I'm critical because I know some of these companies should have already invested in improving their digital properties' UX by now.

People talk about how Amazon is eating the retail world (and this was especially true during the COVID-19 lockdowns), but many other retailers had *plenty of time* before that crisis to move into the digital world and offer some real competition to Amazon. Some, such as Walmart, Best Buy, Target, and Home Depot, actually have. Some have not and are paying the price. According to *Digital Commerce 360,*

> Amazon alone represented nearly a third—31.4%—of all U.S. ecommerce sales growth in 2020. That's certainly a significant share of online sales growth, and one we're familiar with when it comes to the ecommerce giant, but there's more to the story. The 31.4% is down from Amazon's 43.8% share in 2019. This is likely a sign of the gains made by other big competitors in 2020.[9]

So I'm critical of those who haven't been visionaries and innovators, but at the same time, I'm also very sympathetic to some companies that aren't able to fully adapt to the digital world. It's often because they lack knowledge or resources, but it is also because of how difficult it is to build and deliver a great digital experience. For example, it's certainly challenging for a mom-and-pop store to go digital and provide such an experience: it's expensive, and they have limited resources. It requires a combination of excellent technology, design, and customer insights that provide a road map to creating a great digital experience. It would be wonderful if all businesses could offer a great digital experience, but it's not that easy to make it happen.

And that's why I've written this book—because the more you know about what makes an excellent UX and how to go about developing it, the less time it will take you to achieve it. A universally applicable way to improve the UX is to gather insights about it directly from users, which can come from UX research or other forms of data. If the end user of a digital product or a website is going to experience problems or frustrations using the product, it's important to

---

9   Fareeha Ali, "US Ecommerce Grows 44.0% in 2020," *Digital Commerce 360*, January 29, 2021 https://www.digitalcommerce360.com/article/us-ecommerce-sales/.

uncover them—to "de-risk" the project—as early as possible in the development process. You can conduct usability testing over different approaches and/or versions, iterate and quickly see which is more successful. Usability testing is a technique used in user-centered inter-action design to evaluate a product by testing it on users. It is more concerned with the design intuitiveness of the product and tested with users who have no prior exposure to it. Such testing is paramount to the success of an end product, as a fully functioning application that creates confusion among its users will not last for long. The beauty of testing even with a few users is that it can quickly lead to a new iteration, which can be tested again, until you get the desired results.

This seems like a lot of testing, but today the cost of doing UX research and usability testing has come down dramatically with the ability to use the Internet and automate a good part of it with software tools. Not long ago, most testing was done in person in special facili-ties, but this dramatic shift to using technology has really sped the process up. With this automated approach, most of the instruction to test subjects is delivered digitally, and they can speak and be recorded, so their responses can be studied by the design and development team members to improve UX. These tools allow more iterative testing that can start earlier in the development process. It can be done within a few hours, which allows companies to test much more frequently than they did before—sometimes doing ten studies a month easily and sometimes testing *daily!* We will cover UX research and user testing in chapters 4 and 5.

There are multiple types of software testing. The goal of software testing is to determine if the requirements were met and all the use cases were covered without technical errors. Usability testing focuses on how well the technology supports what the user wants to do. Usability testing uncovers the *how* and the *why* behind the *what*—which is the kind of understanding you need to make a digital experience success-ful. You need to understand how and why your customers interact with your digital brand the way they do. What's their motivation? What do they need to know? What are their expectations coming in? What do they like? What frustrates them? What satisfies them?

Say UPS wants to know how users respond when they do not get a package the company says was delivered. In their research, they would ask users to go to the UPS website and try to find out why they didn't receive the package and what they can do about it. Then they would watch where the users go on the website and what they do and how the experience affects them. Was it easy or frustrating to get to the information required? Was that information clear? If they had to go somewhere else on the website to get what they wanted, was it clear where to go and what to do when they got there? Answers to such questions will help shape a better design that will create a truly customer-centric experience.

Great UX + Great CX = Business Success

A personal experience I had with Grubhub points to the fact that the UX is just a starting point for the CX, and how both need to work well for a great total experience. One Friday evening, my very hungry ten-year-old was craving a good pizza, so I headed over to … my iPhone, of course! As Papa John's no longer delivers in my area, I really needed to look for an alternative, pronto. Fortunately, I'd heard about Grubhub, so I went ahead and started a brand-new journey, a totally new experience, with their app, hoping it would save me from the wrath of my "hangry" child!

Grubhub has a great UX design. You can recognize a great UX because it's "invisible," meaning that usually we only pay attention to UX design when it's poor and therefore causes us difficulty. If you can simply do what you came to do in an effortless, fast, and pleasant way, it's a great UX design. Thanks to the Grubhub app's great design and content, in about five minutes I was able to

- quickly sign up as a new user (using one of my Google account's SSO logins);

- configure my profile (basic preferences, address, and payment method);

- easily search and select a nearby pizza restaurant (I picked Round Table Pizza);

- efficiently customize the pizza with an easy-to-use, step-by-step workflow; and

- order the pizza.

I even bought a subscription to Grubhub on the spot, because doing so lowered the cost of my deliveries, and I liked the convenience of the app. So far, so good—in fact, an excellent UX indeed.

Once the order was confirmed, the app estimated a twenty-five- to thirty-five-minute delivery time. That's totally normal and expected on a Friday night, so I went ahead and reported the good news to my son, making myself a small-time parental hero. Then, things went sour.

First, the pizza arrived sixty-five minutes after the order was placed, not twenty-five to thirty-five minutes as the app had estimated—*and I wasn't notified about this delay at any point.* Being a little late is acceptable on a Friday night, but doubling the original estimated delivery time without any notice is *not* acceptable!

Next, and much worse, when the pizza finally arrived, it was the wrong one! I opened the box in the kitchen in front of my hungry ten-year-old, and he was *not happy*—believe me! But I was able to hurry out to the driveway to let the driver know what had happened and try to salvage the situation. His reply stunned me: "Sir, I'm from Grubhub. I only deliver what Round Table Pizza gives me. So you need to deal with them from this point on." Then he drove away, erasing any resemblance I might have had, just sixty minutes before, to a hero dad.

The initial Grubhub UX was great. Because of that, the digital interaction with the app made a great impression on me, made me a fan of the Grubhub brand. But this nice digital UX was just 50 percent of the total experience. Once I became a customer, the CX went all wrong. The pizza was late, it was the wrong kind, and the driver, a representative of the Grubhub brand, took no responsibility for the error and made no effort to make things right.

Later, I wrote a feedback note using the Grubhub app, explaining the situation in great detail, because I was really upset about it. You would think that, in this megacompetitive pizza market, as well as the crowded food-delivery-app market, *someone* would have contacted me to offer me an apology and, at the very least, some credit toward the next order. (I guess I'm used to Amazon.com's standards.) But no. Instead, ironically, *every week* since that experience, I've been getting suggestions from Grubhub to *repeat this screwed-up order*! The final score—UX one, CX zero. Because of this discrepancy, I am much more skeptical about the Grubhub brand than I originally was.

The UX is basically the emotions and feelings that the user experiences while interacting with your company's products or services. Whether it's a bad UX experience, just an okay one, a good one, or a *great* one is going to directly impact whether or not that user will turn into a consumer and will want to use your website or app again and whether he or she will recommend it to others. The power of a great UX *and* CX *working together* cannot be underestimated in our increasingly digital world.

In summary, UI, CX, and UX are different, but they're very closely related:

- **UI** is what users see when they first encounter digitally the presentation of your product, service, or brand. It's how things look, what kind of feeling they convey, and where menus and linked lists and so on are located on the screen. It's about what meets the user's eye and where their eye leads them, what kind of choice and direction it offers.

- **UX** is the total experience a user has when interacting with your digital presence. In order to develop it effectively, you need to focus on, in a more proactive way, things such as product design and usability—before the product or service or website is developed and then launched. To measure it, you need to unlock insights derived from task success rates, efficiency rates, and the System Usability Scale (SUS) as well as why and how (behavioral data) users do what they do.

- **CX** focuses on satisfaction and other attitudinal metrics, such as NPS (Net Promoter Score) and other ratings, typically collected through surveys, and it's measured after the product launch phase.

Whether it's a bad UX experience, just an okay one, a good one, or a *great* one is going to directly impact whether or not that user will turn into a consumer and will want to use your website or app again.

UX, while being a different discipline from CX, greatly benefits from knowing the customer and the customer life cycle. CX teams should form a close partnership with UX teams in order to provide this customer insight and to help innovate touchpoints.

The kinds of activities in UX are mostly done by product management, engineering, and design, whereas the items under CX are often done by marketing. The chance for working in silos and not coordinating is high. But ultimately, *CX and UX need to work together in order to deliver a great overall experience.* Period. It's not about user *or* customer. It's about both. It's about the overall experience. The way I experienced Grubhub started with an ad, then moved on to the product (the app), and then it was one of their employees, and finally with Round Table Pizza's product (the wrong pizza). All of these touchpoints contributed to the overall experience I had with Grubhub.

As I said at the outset of this chapter, every company is a digital experience company—or should soon be. Most interactions with a brand will be through digital channels; therefore companies will need to focus on the design of their digital properties. User research will play a huge role, because great experiences will require deep understanding of the end user and the customer. In the next chapter, I'll discuss why this is the moment for companies to seize the opportunity to establish a strong digital brand in the world.

─────── KEY TAKEAWAYS ───────

▶ In order to survive and thrive, you *must* recognize that, now and forever, *all companies are digital experience companies*. The sooner you understand this and create a strategy that takes advantage of it, the more likely you are to be successful.

▶ Just having a digital *presence* isn't enough; in order to succeed in our increasingly digital world, your website or app *must produce a great experience* for customers and potential customers. Being a digital experience company means being a totally customer-centric company.

▶ A Forrester report on the business impact of good design in customer interfaces shows that companies who focus on good UX and CX design experience benefits such as greater customer loyalty, increased revenue, a higher market valuation, and better-performing stock.

▶ The power of a great UX *and* CX *working together* cannot be underestimated in our increasingly digital world.

▶ UX research and user testing is one of the keys to the successful development of your digital presence. UX research uncovers the how and the why behind the what of your users' and customers' experience of that presence.

CHAPTER 2

The Best of Times, the Worst of Times

It was the best of times, it was the worst of times, it was the age of wisdom, it was the age of foolishness.... It was the season of darkness, it was the spring of hope ...
—CHARLES DICKENS, *A TALE OF TWO CITIES*

I f you have a great UX design, backed up by a great overall CX, this is the best of times for your business. Given the right market conditions, you can grow like crazy and reap great profits. Your online experience can absolutely provide you with a significant advantage over competitors who don't take those elements as seriously. The scale of what you can do today—nationally and internationally—in our digital era has no parallel in history. The reach of the Internet is almost unlimited. It doesn't matter where you're located. It often doesn't require a marketing and sales team (a concept called "product-led growth," which I discuss later in the book). Through a great digital experience, you can win new adopters by word of mouth—people sharing their good experiences with their friends and families, tech or niche magazines writing about it, and so on. You can also retain those customers year after year and reduce "churn," or subscription cancellations, arguably the most important metric for any SaaS business. The great experience you provide is a force multiplier for the marketing, sales, and account management efforts—and the sky's the limit!

There is a kind of 1849 California Gold Rush feeling to the digital era we're living in. If you can design, develop, and deliver a product or service that is easy to use and fills a market need, you can succeed more quickly and to a greater extent than has ever been possible.

One of the changes driving such success is a change in business buying practices in B2B (business-to-business) enterprise software. It used to be that the buyer was often not the user. A company would purchase an enterprise-wide license negotiated by the purchasing department for a product or service. And there are advantages to that: economies of scale. But over the last ten years, we've seen a growth in the capacity for the end users to be the buyers instead of having the purchasing department make the decision for them.

Employees, teams, and departments want to make such decisions based on how they like a product or service. With digital products and services, it's much easier to try them out and decide, and because so much is SaaS, subscriptions can be taken for a very limited time and canceled if the product or service is unsatisfactory. These products are so much easier to test out and so much cheaper to buy that people can make those decisions for themselves. They might choose and purchase a product or service, and the purchasing department doesn't even *know* about it until later, because the cost of the product or service was within the user's discretionary budget—under the company limit for an individual or team or department purchases—and because it was relatively inexpensive, they were able to buy it with a credit card. This concept is known as the "consumerization of enterprise software."[10]

And once again, this takes us back to the idea of this being the best of times for digital companies, because users want to try out the product or service for a time and, if they like it, buy it and keep on using it and spread the word about it. But if you want this to happen with your product or service, you'd better produce a great UX that will convince the end user to make the purchase. Because if you don't, they're not going to buy after they try, and/or they will cancel their subscription after they buy for a limited period and find something else that works for them. This is a fundamental change in user behavior that makes a great UX the key to success in the business application world. It will directly impact how much new business you will sell and how much business you will retain.

If, on the other hand, you don't have great UX design, or if you're not even solidly planted in the digital world yet—these are the worst of times. You may soon face, or may already be facing, a competitor who has boiled down what you offer to digital products and services that are easier to access and use than yours are. *And the kicker is that this may be true even if your products or services provide more value than your competitors!*

Focusing now on B2C (business-to-consumer) products, in this digital era, the end users want simple, convenient, intuitive experiences. There was a time when they were willing to consult a user manual, accepted a learning

If you don't have great UX design, or if you're not even solidly planted in the digital world yet—these are the worst of times.

---

10   Jay Kappor, "Consumerization of Enterprise Software—Part 1," Medium, August 27, 2019, https://medium.com/jaykapoornyc/consumerization-of-enterprise-software-part-i-7b48274889f6.

curve to figure out how to use a product or service. But no more. If your competitor's product or service has a better UX, if it's more intuitive and easier to use, potential customers will choose it over yours and your customers *will* switch. This is particularly true of SaaS businesses, because it's so easy for the consumer to make the switch and cancel a subscription. Precisely because it's so easy to change vendors, these are times when delivering great experience is a huge part of your overall competitive advantage. Have no doubt, great UX design will make your product stickier. This is particularly true in commodity or highly fragmented markets, where it becomes harder and harder to differentiate your business or brand from the competition. I'm talking about vertical markets like banking, travel, or retail. Users don't expect to put time into learning how to use your product or service anymore; they expect *you* to make using it easy for them. And that's what great UX design does.

There's never been a better time to build and market a software product. There's never been a time when it was easier to distribute and grow such a product. And because of this, there's never been an easier time to create economies of scale and have great gross margins. The efficiency of digital businesses is unbelievable, due to automation. So there's never been a better time to enjoy the benefits from all this—it *is* the best of times. But you will never be able to benefit, to get a high return on your investment, unless you have great UX design.

So the choice is yours. Do you want to live in the best of times or the worst of times?

Digital Disruption

Many markets have been, are being, or soon *will be* disrupted by digital products and services that enable consumers to do things more easily digitally. Uber is a good example from the pre-COVID-19 world.

(COVID hit them hard not because there was any problem with their UX but because people couldn't get into cars with strangers.) They made it incredibly easy to locate and procure individual transportation—instantly and relatively inexpensively.

It wasn't that cabs didn't exist. They'd existed for a century and half! But they had become very expensive in most cities, and cab companies were often a bit lackadaisical about customer service. After all, they had a monopoly on "reasonably priced" individual transportation, because the alternative, hiring a private car, was even *more* expensive.

Along comes Uber with a very clear and simple app that locates the nearest car that matches your needs, lets you communicate directly with the driver, lets you pay online, and costs *a lot less* than a cab. It was stunning how fast Uber took over a market that cab companies had *owned* for a century and a half. All because of a smart concept and a great UX that made it easier and cheaper for end users to get instant transportation.

Car dealerships are another business that has been around for a long time. But the selling and buying of cars has now gone digital, too, and who knows how long "tire kicking" at dealerships will continue to happen. Dealerships sometimes try the online approach, but from a UX design perspective, they're usually not very successful. Not being digital technology companies, they often buy prepackaged e-commerce applications that just don't make the grade.

Contrast that with the custom, purpose-built websites/apps presented by companies such as Cars.com and CarGurus.com, companies that were built

It was stunning how fast Uber took over a market that cab companies had *owned* for a century and a half.

digitally and have been working on their digital channel and have invested in UX design for years. They allow the consumer to do the things they want to do when they buy a car better and more easily than they can when they have to work with a dealer.

I've actually bought two cars online in the past four years. I never thought I'd buy a car online—you have to kick the tires, right? But it turns out that these digital car sellers are good at letting you kick tires virtually. Let's start with filtering. These companies offer a huge number of variables that let you narrow down your search to exactly what you want—and you don't have to wander the car lot with a salesman breathing down your neck to find it. You're not limited to one or two brands of cars, either, as you are at a dealership. Then there are pictures—lots of pictures—that give you a clear sense of each car, what it looks like, and what its features are. The consumer feels like the proverbial kid in the candy store! Then there are specs and reviews, which further clarify what you're buying.

In short, when you use these digital sellers, it feels like *you're buying* a car—it's customer centric—but when you go to most dealerships, it feels like *they're trying to sell you* a car. The other thing these sites do is arm consumers who do decide to go to a dealership with the kind of information they need to get the best deal. However you go about it, thanks to these well-designed digital car-buying UXs, there's no longer any need to fly blind when you're purchasing a car.

Over the last decade, consumers have gravitated toward digital channels and companies. Some of it is generational, but there are plenty of older people using Uber and Lyft and Autotrader and Car Gurus—and Hotels.com and Airbnb.com and many other digital companies. Consumers like having relationships with such companies, even though those companies are just efficient intermediaries—they don't own cabs or dealerships full of cars or hotels or bed-and-breakfasts or any of the end products these users are seeking. They just have digital applications that make it easier for consumers to get what they want in these areas.

Meeting a user need in a better way is what ultimately drives disruption to an industry like taxicabs, and the easy-to-use UX is what fuels the velocity of that transformation. In the case of Uber, the company disrupted the taxi industry by addressing five user needs that were totally unmet by taxis:

1. Finding/ordering a ride easily, based on where you are right now

2. Knowing the cost and time to get there before committing

3. Ensuring you are going the right way and not getting a runaround to jack up the fare

4. Incentivizing the driver (and rider) to be good with a mutual rating system.

5. Removing the pain of paying for the ride by integrating it into the app

These five unmet needs in taxis are what set up the potential for Uber and Lyft to disrupt the taxi industry. Then the good UX that went into building the Uber and Lyft apps helped fuel their adoption and growth. If they had implemented a solution that met the above needs but not in an intuitive, easy-to-use way, they well might have disrupted the industry but not at the speed they did. This might have given the taxi industry a chance to respond. So the key to technological disruption is not only having a great idea that better meets a user need but also building it in a way (a great UX) that allows that transformation to happen quickly to change an industry almost overnight.

So this is why we're in the best of times for companies that get it right. They can grow in popularity and adoptions like crazy over a short period of time. But at the same time, if you don't wake up, if you're an incumbent in your industry and don't understand what it takes to digitally transform your business, the right way to shape your UI and UX, it's going to be the worst of times.

Great UX as the Main Competitive Advantage

The COVID-19 pandemic lockdowns shined a spotlight on what digital products and services can provide. The success of many companies that had already been doing well in the digital era exploded during the pandemic. Even though the pandemic has been the worst crisis in a hundred years, these companies thrived. On the other hand, companies that hadn't invested in their digital brand, hadn't transformed themselves digitally, had to do it the hard way, catch up fast, just to survive. Many of them didn't. It was not a pretty picture.

You need to think creatively about presenting your products or services through a powerful UX. TripActions is a company that has harnessed the power of a great digital UX to both save companies money on their travel expenses and reward the employees who contribute to their reduction in travel expenses. Here is how it works. An employee who has to go on a business trip is given a budget by the company and uses TripActions's great UX to easily consider travel options: flight, hotel, car, etc. TripActions makes it really easy to search for these things. And then TripActions gives the employee options to choose from. If the employee books travel arrangements that are below budget, part

You need to think creatively about presenting your products or services through a powerful UX.

of those savings are passed on to them by their company. It's a win-win situation. The employee wins by getting a cash benefit, and the company wins by reducing travel expenses.

And because employees make their own travel plans, companies save the expense of using a travel agency too. *However, this would not work if booking the travel was a big hassle for employees.* But TripActions's great UX makes it easy enough that employees enjoy the convenience of flying when and with which airline they want to, staying where they prefer to stay, driving the car they like to drive, and so on. We've been using TripActions at my company, UserZoom, and in just the first year, we saved approximately $100,000 in travel expenses!

Namely is another company that is disrupting the B2B world, this time with an HR application that, once again, empowers employees. With Namely, you take a lot of work out of the hands of the HR department that is really about employees doing their own thing. Maybe an employee needs to download a paid-time-off (PTO) report. Maybe they need to know their stock options. Maybe they need to request time off from their manager. Maybe the manager needs to create a review of that employee. Maybe the employee needs access to the company directory. There are so many things people in a company need to do that don't really have to go through the HR department—and Namely makes them all available digitally via a great, easy-to-use interface.

HR systems are so often old fashioned and slow and hard to use. And then here comes this UX-design-focused company that says, "We're going to make this all a breeze to use, happy, and easy—almost fun." They're revolutionizing the way HR is dealt with in companies—and UX design is the vehicle that is carrying them to that achievement.

This kind of thing is happening with healthcare companies such as Anthem Blue Cross Blue Shield too. They had old-school, highly complex, superprivate systems for decades. But now, people want greater access to their healthcare information and to do more healthcare tasks online, so these companies have had to go digital, building intuitive websites and apps that customers can easily access but that are also secure. Now their customers can see their health records anytime. They can schedule a checkup or a flu shot or a test themselves or send a message to their doctor.

These companies knew this would be fine for young people, who are used to navigating online, but many of their customers are older people who aren't so technically savvy. So when these companies designed the UX for their websites, they had to do research with older people to make sure that the website UX was easy to understand, navigate, and use.

They had to sit these people down in front of the website and ask them questions (to name just a few):

- What is the first thing you want to see when the website comes up?

- Why would you want to see that?

- What is most important for you to be able to access quickly?

- What is the most difficult task you encounter as you use the website?

- Can you make an appointment with a doctor easily?

- Is it easy for you to find where you can pay online?

And so on. By doing this research, these companies were able to design easy-to-use websites that make dealing with healthcare needs significantly easier for their customers.

These questions hint at the approach required to develop a great UI design, UX, and CX. In the next and subsequent chapters, I will lay out in detail some great tips on what you need to do to design a great UX and to make your company truly a digital experience company—one that can take advantage of the best of times.

I now want to tell you the story of how I met Eric Yuan, founder and CEO at Zoom Video Communications. Zoom, the megapopular videoconferencing tool, is a great example of how focusing on the end user experience and customer happiness, with a simple and intuitive UI and UX design, can help a company become wildly successful and outperform its competitors in a matter of just a few years.

At a time when it was considered already a pretty saturated market, Eric founded Zoom back in 2013 to compete against the likes of Webex (a Cisco company) and GoToMeeting (a Citrix product), among many others. I've had the pleasure to know Eric pretty much since those early years at Zoom. He was actually the VP of engineering at Webex and built the product that Cisco ended up buying in 2007. Being a GoToMeeting user myself for many years, I must admit that I had my own reservations on whether there was space in the market for another player. And I wasn't alone. Many in the business media wondered the same thing. After all, what else could Zoom bring to the table?

I remember one day back in 2016 trying Zoom out for the first time from my office in downtown San Jose, California, the so-called heart of Silicon Valley. Eric himself volunteered to do a product demo for me. His office was literally across the street from mine on Almaden Boulevard, right next to Adobe's HQ. I could literally see Eric's office from my window! It was 2016, and remote meetings were not as common as they are today, so I figured I could simply walk over and meet him at his office for the demo. Yet he insisted on doing it remotely, of course!

The demo went really well, and I vividly remember two things that stood out for me:

1. Eric showed up with a warm smile, a light-blue Zoom T-shirt, and a supercool background of the Golden Gate Bridge. He had introduced virtual backgrounds to the videoconference experience, and that immediately made an impact on me. That was different and cool.

2. The UI of the product was spectacularly minimalistic and lean. So easy to use (especially compared to Webex or GoTo-Meeting)—it loaded pretty much instantly—even my five-year-old daughter and ninety-year-old grandma could use it. Eventually, they would …).

Two things happened pretty shortly after that demo. We bought a license, and I went out to lunch with Eric to discuss entrepreneurial stuff, such as working with engineering teams and focusing on the usability of our digital applications. I'll always remember his comment on the importance of great UX design: "To me, great design and app usability is the responsibility of everyone in product, starting with our engineers, not just the designers. A great engineer should also be good at design. It makes no sense to me otherwise." I remember thinking that in most cases that's not what ends up happening. Engineering teams are focused more on the technical details of their products, the architecture and its scalability and the like. They often see having a good UX as the job of the designer or product manager, and so you end up needing designers and researchers to help build a great digital product. He understood that and since then has added these profiles to the team as the company scaled, but he made his engineering team focus on UX from the very beginning, from the MVP (minimum viable product) stage. And I truly believe that this great UX, together with other factors, such as its modern architecture (Cisco left Webex untouched for several years after they acquired it in 2007), was instrumental to Zoom's eventually becoming a phenomenon. It all starts with the leadership team and that relentless focus on the user experience and customer happiness.

By the way, Eric and I remain good friends today, we at UserZoom are a remote company and have been using Zoom and many of their products ever since 2016, and I have the deepest respect for everything Eric has accomplished—most importantly as one of the most humane leaders of our time.

KEY TAKEAWAYS

- ► If you have a great UI design, provide a great UX, and back it up with a great CX, they can provide you with a significant advantage over competitors who don't take those elements as seriously.

- ► Especially with the growth of SaaS, we've seen a significant increase in the capacity for the end users, instead of purchasing agents, to be the buyers—and it is a great UX that convinces them to buy, use, and renew.

► You may soon face, or may already be facing, a competitor who has boiled down what you offer to digital products and/ or services that are easier to access and use than yours are.

► If you're an incumbent in your industry and don't understand what it takes to digitally transform your business, it's going to be the worst of times.

► Think creatively, reconsider how to present your products and services to the market, and potentially go outside of your comfort zone. Start by asking lots of questions and getting to know your users' needs and preferences. Focus on delivering a powerful UX that makes is easy and convenient for your users to interact with you.

CHAPTER 3

Easy Is Hard

Everything is hard before it is easy.
—JOHANN WOLFGANG VON GOETHE

I t's not as if there are companies that *don't* want to provide a great digital experience. There's no resistance to doing that. Everybody wants to do it. It's the same with UX testing and research. Everybody would *love* to find out if what they're going to build or offer to the market is working well before they release it. The big challenge, and what prevents a lot of companies from achieving this, is that it's actually hard to execute. Really hard. It's like going to war, not like playing a game of chess—and if you see it as chess, you're probably going to fail at it and/or be defeated by your competitors. The results of a survey conducted by McKinsey & Company show that only 10 percent of CEOs reported realizing design's full potential, a result driven primarily by a lack of clarity as to how design leaders can contribute and uncertainty about what to expect of them in their role.[11]

11   Melissa Dalrymple et al., "Are you asking enough from your design leaders?" McKinsey, February 19, 2020, https://www.mckinsey.com/business-functions/ mckinsey-design/our-insights/are-you-asking-enough-from-your-design-leaders.

A recent study conducted by *Chief Executive* magazine shows that nearly half of CEOs struggle with digitalization efforts.[12] When it comes to winning in this new era for business, CEOs across virtually every industry in every part of the nation agree on two things:

1. Becoming a more digitally sophisticated enterprise is essential.

2. They are struggling to make it happen.

Those are two of the key takeaways from a new survey of CEOs conducted by *Chief Executive* in May 2021 as part of a new initiative to help the nation's C-suites become better digital leaders. When it comes to becoming a more digitally innovative company, the research found that 70 percent of CEOs say their organization is in full swing with various stages of digitalization initiatives.

Yet nearly half of the CEOs polled (47 percent) responded that when it comes to leading a digitally innovative company, they either feel like they are "hanging in there" or are simply "out of their depth."

Furthermore, 36 percent report being deeply committed to innovation, with a strategy and plan in place, and 34 percent say they are on the innovation journey, with initiatives planned across the organization. Further, 28 percent say things are also in progress for them on that front but that initiatives are only taking place in certain areas of the organization. Lastly, only 2 percent of the 239 CEOs surveyed say they have not yet started or are working on getting started but need help.

The effort is essential. When asked to rate the degree to which innovation drives every action at their company, CEOs polled gave it a 6.9 out of 10 on our 10-point scale.

Among the challenges to innovation are

---

12   "Nearly Half of CEOs Struggling with Digitalization Efforts, Poll Finds," *Chief Executive*, June 15, 2021, https://chiefexecutive.net/nearly-half-of-ceos-struggling-with-digitalization-efforts-poll-finds/.

- talent (38 percent),

- prioritization (24 percent), and

- culture (21 percent).

It is not surprising to find companies, particularly traditional companies, struggling with not having the right talent, time, or culture to drive innovation. Or if they do have the talent that can help digital innovation efforts, they struggle to find ways to best empower them to boldly innovate.

Over the years, I've personally seen a lot of top executives who didn't understand the importance of investing in the design and testing resources required to develop a killer digital UX. They understood the importance of the back-end infrastructure—the software, servers, hardware, data security, etc.—but they gave short shrift to the front-end design. Which is ironic, if you think about it, because their potential customers *never even paid attention nor cared about the back end.* They sort of just took all of that for granted. Why is that? you may wonder. One possibility is that without a back end, there is no product. It is very possible to build a service without a good front-end experience, and it can be shipped, so the box gets checked. But you cannot build a product with just a front end and not back end. What potential customers did see, and what represented these companies to them, was the front end—the quality of UI and UX and how convenient and easy it was to use. This, I guarantee you, is something customers care a whole lot about.

Many executives are perfectly comfortable allocating large sums of money for the back-end e-commerce technology as well as the engineering resources but balk at spending real money on front-end design and testing. Their naive, old-fashioned, software engineering–based attitude is, "Give me a solid back end and paint a picture on the front of it for the user," as if creating the front end is just icing on the infrastructure cake. But this is simply not true. A product design has three different aspects, all of which must be taken into account and tested: function, visual appeal, and interactivity. Each of these areas is important and quite complicated in itself, and we'll talk about each of them at length later, but they must be taken into consideration in order to create a great overall UX.

Imagine if Apple, when it developed its revolutionary personal computer, had only focused on engineering. They did—and do—have great engineering behind their products. But when they went to Xerox PARC and saw the mouse, the GUI (graphical user interface), and the icon-based interface that had been developed there, they understood that it was *the ability to interact easily with the machine* that was going to change personal computing. They built an interface that was just as important as their infrastructure, the technology within the machine, and revolutionized the personal computer. In fact, one might say that computers were not *truly* personal until Apple recognized the importance of the interface and invested in doing something about it.

Steve Jobs had a very clear vision of the value of design. He was frequently quoted: "Design is not how it looks but how it works." And yet decades later, some businesspeople still have a hard time seeing that they need to be as committed to investing in great user interface design and in testing the UX as they are to building a solid infrastructure. Companies with this kind of attitude are doomed to failure in an increasingly digital world. The current revolution in digital experience is similar to what Apple did for the personal computer—and it is having an equally revolutionary effect.

To give just one example, compare Airbnb to a standard hotel website. The hotel interface is usually clunky and limited in functionality, while Airbnb's is fun, easy to use, and provides lots of options to solve real users' problems, such as searching for a place, viewing quality photographs (in fact, it was incorporating high-quality photos that initially increased Airbnb's appeal tremendously), reading reviews of those places, saving favorites, and so on. This is why Airbnb succeeded so quickly and is now a public company worth over $100 billion, versus Hilton, for instance, which is worth $32 billion.

This front-end UX emphasis has caught a lot of businesspeople off guard. Insurance companies and banks made huge investments in the back end, but the UI was almost an afterthought, one that was often put in the hands of engineers—who are *not* UX designers. This approach will not work anymore. The back end is somewhat of a commodity now, but the front end is always unique. It's where the rubber meets the road, where the consumer and then (you hope) the customers interact with your brand and are convinced—or not convinced—to work with your company, to use your app or service.

For instance, the old, staid Barclays bank shook off the dust and designed what has become the most popular banking app in England— and they get UX feedback from users constantly so they can continually improve it. UX design requires a whole different skill set than engineering. A good UX has to be backed by good technology, of course, but it also demands tremendous creative expertise from designers, user researchers, copywriters, marketing specialists, and so on.

If you're not willing to make the full investment in your front end, you're toast in today's economy! The pandemic made this abundantly clear. It pushed the need for an engaging and convenient digital experience to the forefront, accelerated the need for it. *But* I and many others saw the need for this emphasis on UX coming for a long time; it was just happening in slow motion, relatively speaking, before the pandemic. Today, everybody expects to use the digital interface of a product to get things done—and they expect you to make it easy and enjoyable for them to do those things. This expectation did not start with the pandemic or end with the pandemic; it's part of the culture now. Companies who had been making this change already, who had been responding to this revolution in the importance of the digital UX, prospered even during the pandemic, and they will continue to prosper well into the future—because this *is* the wave of the future, part of the "new normal," and won't likely go away post–pandemic times.

By the way, as I discussed in the previous chapter, this is true not just for B2C (business-to-consumer) companies but for B2B (business-to-business) enterprises as well. In order to be a successful digital experience company, you need to have both an enterprise-grade back end and a consumer-grade front end. As we will see in chapter 7, the benefits of great UX design are equally valuable to both. If you've been caught off guard by this revolution, it is essential for you to wake up and fully appreciate what's going on. If you missed the boat the first time around, you need to recognize that and admit how important it is to get on that boat. You have to invest in the necessary resources and strategies to avoid missing the boat again. The purpose of this book is to inspire you to invest in great UX design and to guide you in doing it effectively.

Designing the Digital Experience That You Need

When a potential customer encounters your website or app, you usually want them to be able to do a variety of things: search for your products, learn about those products, compare your products to others in the industry, make an informed decision about which products they want, buy the products, share their experience with people they know, and ultimately continue using the products because they're having a great experience with them. And that experience can include many different activities at different times: interacting with the products, customizing them, exploring their various features, performing tasks, sharing them, and so on. Making all of this interactivity happen on the limited real estate of a computer screen or tablet computer screen, and making it happen in an engaging and relatively easy way, is incredibly complicated.

And those are the big screens! These days, more and more people are doing everything they can on their phones—a tiny screen on which to make those multiple complicated things happen! Imagine a company such as Home Depot or Lowe's trying to make millions of products and services available in this format. Or a financial company trying to make it convenient for users to get to and use hundreds of financial products and services without consulting with a financial agent. I've been in UX design for over twenty years, and I can tell you that it's a major headache figuring out how to make this work.

And this takes me back to the original point I made in this chapter. Easy is hard. Having data about the user behavior is relatively easy for a website, mobile app, or desktop software with telemetry built in. But these metrics don't tell you if (a) the experience is easy, and (b) if the experience is valuable/useful. That's where UX research helps fill the need, both quantitatively and now qualitatively. And if you don't acknowledge how important—and difficult—it is to design a great UX, you'll never make the investment necessary to get it right. A lot of companies are finally getting this today, but many of them have gotten it the hard way, not going into this effort with a sense of what it's going to require and being blindsided by the difficulty and expense—and by the extent of the investment in design. Companies need to know how to organize themselves so that they can be effective and efficient in the way they build these digital experiences. It's more important than ever to hire a design leader and provide them with a seat at the table, at the same level as the engineering leader, and assume total responsibility over the task of front-end interaction and visual design

The design leader is the person who is in charge of making the UX—which is the way consumers are going to experience the company—great: engaging, easy to use, effective, and efficient. Apple is a great example of this way of thinking. They don't just produce some of the most technically sophisticated products, the most visually beautiful, but also the most intuitive and easy-to-use products. As Steve Jobs would say, "You have to start with the user experience and work your way backward." They give the UX attention equal to that given the technology. Their design team is just as strong as (if not stronger than) their engineering team—and that's the reason they're so successful.

If you don't acknowledge how important—and difficult—it is to design a great UX, you'll never make the investment necessary to get it right.

Now, it's important to note that Apple's design team is strong because Steve Jobs personally decided it would be. He held the experience quality as the highest and most important goal to achieve at the company. This is just not true for many companies. Leadership is simply not as design focused as Jobs was. In most cases, for design teams to be effective, they need to invest in UX research to help them make informed decisions based on real human feedback.

Design skills are something engineers don't necessarily have—in fact, they are very unlikely to have them. They're great with the back end, but the front end requires a different type of creative work and understanding of human behavior. It's a different set of

46

skills. Companies that understand this are appointing design leaders who understand UX and visual and functional design and product managers who understand and can deal with design requirements—in short, they're baking good design into the product from the start of the process, not at the end. It's essential to have solid and experienced digital design expertise in order to create a successful front end.

It's no accident that many of the most successful digital companies were well aware of the importance of design from the start. Steve Jobs had a design background. Brian Chesky, founder and CEO of Airbnb, has a design background. Some companies have design executives now: a chief experience officer, chief design officer, or VP of design. At my own company, UserZoom, we have a VP of design who reports to the COO, and the person in that position has a major impact on what we produce and how we present it to the end users. In a 2017 Design Council article about the importance of a chief design office, James Pallister reported that

> as Apple's valuation shot higher and higher in recent years, a flurry of major corporations—Philips, PepsiCo, Hyundai—announced the appointments of Chief Design Officers to their boards.
>
> This was no mere coincidence. Seeking to emulate the stellar success of design-led businesses like Apple, global companies are pouring investment into design. IBM, for one, announced a $100 million investment in its design capabilities last year, with the aim to hire 1,000 designers across its global workforce by 2018.
>
> The twentieth century marketing perspective of "making people want things" has transitioned to a twenty-first century approach of "making things people want," and design—with

its focus on users—is the route through which brands will either succeed or fail.[13]

Forward-looking companies are adding a lot more designers, dramatically changing the designer-to-engineer ratio. In the past, that ratio could easily be one designer per fifty engineers—the emphasis was build, build, build, with not nearly as much emphasis on front-end design. Now, in these forward-looking companies, you'll see much higher ratios of designers to engineers. Even back three years, in the *TechCrunch* article "6 Major Tech Companies Have Doubled Their Design Hiring Goals in the Last Half Decade," Dylan Field noted that IBM had gone from a 1:72 designer-to-engineer ratio to a 1:8 ratio; Atlassian from 1:25 to 1:9; and Dropbox from 1:10 to 1:6 .[14] This is a huge change. And the companies that lead the way with a strong emphasis on design—Amazon, Google, Airbnb, Facebook, and so on—also lead the way in the stock market. So they're not just cool companies; they're financially sound companies, because this approach can truly spur success.

In an article written in August 2020 by Andrew Jones, an experienced Silicon Valley product leader, and titled "Design Is Eating Code, Even as Software Eats the World," Jones highlights that product design today lets builders go faster and further before ever requiring code.[15] It is driving the no-code movement. In building a website or app, only a few early steps used to fall under the "design" category—

---

13   James Pallister, "The Secrets of the Chief Design Officer," Design Council, April 27, 2015. https://www.designcouncil.org.uk/news-opinion/secrets-chief-design-officer-0.

14   Dylan Field, "6 Major Tech Companies Have Doubled Their Design Hiring Goals in Last Half Decade," *TechCrunch*, May 31, 2017, https://techcrunch.com/2017/05/31/here-are-some-reasons-behind-techs-design-shortage/.

15   Andrew Jones, "Design is eating code, even as software eats the world," *UX Collective*, August 5, 2020, https://uxdesign.cc/design-is-eating-code-even-as-software-eats-the-world-f40195982a08.

followed by a much lengthier coding process. Today design can get you much further … in some cases, depending on complexity, all the way to the finish line.

The graphic is oversimplified, but fundamentally this is a tremendous shift in technology and process. Peter Levine (of a16z) wrote earlier this year, "A decade ago, function over presentation was the rule, so you needed a workflow manual just to follow the user interface! But now—in the decade of design—the interface no longer reflects the code; rather, the code reflects the design."[16]

Companies that lead the way with a strong emphasis on design—Amazon, Google, Airbnb, Facebook, and so on—also lead the way in the stock market.

Development Process Before

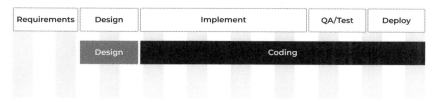

Waterfall development is linear and doesn't emphasize testing or course correcting midstream.

As companies continue to move away from the slow and expensive waterfall methodology in favor of agile development, they inevitably invest more in design. Why? Because it's faster and cheaper. In a word, it's more efficient.

16   Peter Levine, "Investing in Figma: The Decade of Design," Future from a16z, April 30, 2020, https://a16z.com/2020/04/30/figma/.

Development Process Today

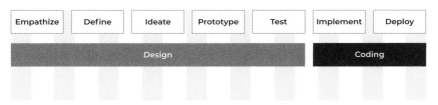

Agile development and design thinking emphasize speed, ideation, and testing—best accomplished by incorporating many more components of product design.

A lot of companies are still evolving in their understanding that designing great experiences is very hard. What they're seeing is that the revolution has started already, and it's going to grow and grow and grow, and they need to be part of it. More and more leaders of companies are changing their strategies to invest significantly in design, because they're coming to realize how hard it is to get it right.

As you go through the process of building a digital product, interface, or overall digital experience, you come to realize that "it takes a village" to produce something really great. You come to see that it's not something that you can just leave in the hands of a self-contained team or a third party and expect them to produce what you need. Producing something like this demands a tremendous level of collaboration within the company and with your users via user testing.

For example, designers might come up with a great idea and then find out from engineering that it's not technologically feasible. (I think of Progressive insurance, which touts the ability to compare their estimate of your premium with those of other insurance companies via their website. I'll bet that when their software engineers first heard that idea, they said something like, "Whoa! That's not easy to do!") Or marketing may come up with something they want to emphasize on a website, and sales will say, "Wait, that's not what sells best for us." Or design may put a function somewhere, but UX testing will reveal that users can't easily find it.

There are literally thousands of small and large decisions involved in designing and executing a digital UX that not only will do what the company needs it to do but is also engaging and easy to use—which, as I've said before, is the baseline user expectation now. And it is not easy to achieve! It takes a village.

What End Users Really Care About

As I said earlier in the book, being digital means being, above all, customer centric—and that, of course, is what a good UX is all about. And as James Pallister said in the previous quote, your job is not to make people want things but to make things people want. So finding out what people want and designing around that is key. Users don't care about your internal struggles over back-end or front-end design and functionality—whether or not marketing gets the blue it wants on the website or whether or not one engineer's approach to coding an app is chosen over another's. They just want an end product that makes their tasks and their lives easier and convenient.

In the industry we call it the "experience gap." What this basically means is that often companies believe they're delivering a great product experience, but the end users actually don't feel the same way. The end user really doesn't care about 99 percent of what's going on when you design and build a website or app. They just care about what they expect it to do for them. They don't care about the challenges that the companies face making these things work. They simply don't care. They're agnostic. All that really matters to them is the quality of the experience, not so much the brand, not so much the company. Obviously, it does matter, but even if you're a famous bank or insurance company or whatever kind of company, they'll cut you off in a minute if you're not meeting their needs, if you're not providing a good user experience for them. They will go with convenience. They will go with ease. They will go with speed. They will go with whatever makes things simple for them. Because they're busy. Because they don't want to read a user manual or have to call customer service. They prefer a self-service option. So companies that are investing in a high-quality digital interface and experience are winning the battle and their customers' loyalty. They're stealing customers away from companies that don't pay enough attention to the quality of the digital experience they provide.

And as I mentioned earlier, easy is hard. It's not *easy* to provide this kind of convenient user experience. Companies are looking for all kinds of ways to ensure their design work is in line with the end user expectations and mental models. As we've covered in the book so far, it has a big impact on both development costs and postlaunch benefits.

I look at it in a simplified way. There are three ways to achieve it:

- You can hire a Steve Jobs–like design genius.

- You can be super lucky and "get it right."

- You can invest in user research and testing and prioritize use of those insights to drive positive change in your product development process.

Most of us aren't Steve Jobs, and few of us would rely on our luck, so that leaves investing in user research and testing. And that's why I've written this book: to make it clear what you need to do and how you need to go about it in order to provide a great digital experience for your users. And it's all about customer centricity and implementing regular, well-designed, iterative user research and testing through-out the entire product development life cycle. Without these, your chances of recouping your considerable investment in developing a digital presence are slim.

Let's start by saying that UX research is not the same as market research. Market research has a broader scope, and often it's done before or after the product has been designed. But UX research and testing are all about making something people want. You bring it into the process as early as possible, so you don't spend a lot of time on things that aren't going to satisfy your users' needs or provide them with a good experience. UX research also focuses a lot more than market research on the *qualitative* aspects of the product experience. You're going to have conversations with the end user. You're going to show them a prototype early in the design process and have them interact with it. And you're going to go through multiple iterations of this process until you get it right, until you've got something that's much more likely to produce a good return on your investment in your digital presence.

Effective UX research should combine what people say *and* do and should be done across both small and large sample sizes to make more strategic decisions. I will provide more details about UX research and testing in the rest of this book.

Traditional Owners

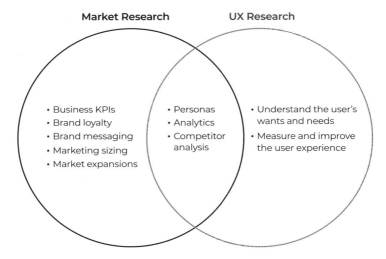

A 2020 SWEOR article conveys how vulnerable a digital experience is to failing. Here are just a handful of the stats it provides:

- It takes about fifty milliseconds (that's 0.05 seconds) for users to form an opinion about your website that determines whether they like your site or not, whether they'll stay or leave.

- 57 percent of Internet users say they won't recommend a business with a poorly designed mobile website.

- 85 percent of adults think that a company's website, when viewed on a mobile device, should be as good or better than its desktop website.

- 38 percent of people will stop engaging with a website if the content or layout is unattractive.

- 88 percent of online consumers are less likely to return to a site after a bad experience.[17]

*Please note that, while in fact an opinion of the quality of the visual design can be made in fifty milliseconds, it isn't what determines if a user will stay or leave. It merely sets the stage for the first interaction. If it's repelling, it's less likely a user will engage but not impossible. If it's inviting, a user will engage, but this alone doesn't guarantee they'll stay. It's what happens in the interaction that determines if they can unlock the value and potential offered

There are twenty-two more statistics in this article, but if these five don't scare you enough to make you take designing and testing your digital platform seriously, you'd better read them again. Doing this right is the key to your company's success in attracting and convincing potential customers in the digital age. One of the purposes of this book is to help you de-risk this process as much as possible—to help you find out as you go along what will work for users and what won't.

UX research and testing has gone through a revolution over the past decade. Companies have always *wanted* to do it, but it's been time consuming and expensive to set up usability test labs and bring people in and have researchers give or moderate the tests. A usability lab is a physical place where usability testing is done, where users are studied interacting with a system for the sake of evaluating the system's usability. The user, or test participant, sits in front of a computer or stands in front of the system's interface alongside a facilitator, or moderator, who gives the user tasks to perform. Behind a one-way mirror, a number of observers watch the interaction, take notes, and ensure the activity is recorded. Very often the testing and the observing room are not placed alongside. In this case the video and audio observation are transmit-

---

17   SWEOR, "27 Eye-Opening Website Statistics," March 5, 2020, https://www.sweor.com/firstimpressions.

ted through a (wireless) network and broadcast via a video monitor or video beamer and loudspeakers. Usually, sessions will be filmed, and the software will log interaction details.[18]

Images of usability labs at SirValUse Consulting GmbH and Xperience Consulting SL.

---

18   "Usability lab," Wikipedia, accessed October 18, 2021, https://en.wikipedia.org/wiki/ Usability_lab.

Companies such as banks, insurance companies, and e-tailers can have hundreds of activities that happen on their sites, so testing each one of these activities in a lab is not easily scalable; it is awfully expensive and time consuming. But UX research automation (or the "cloudification of the lab," as we put it at UserZoom) is enabling a UX research revolution. In the following chapters I will discuss UX research in detail.

With automation, which uses software and the Internet to connect researchers and test participants, companies can manage UX research studies much more efficiently and cost effectively. They can have multiple "virtual labs" operating in the cloud, and each lab can feed its data into the software to help companies get end user feedback and improve their digital UX on an ongoing basis. My company, UserZoom, is one of the companies providing UX research automation, and our goal is to get 80 percent of the testing and data collection process done by software. Essentially, the goal is to spend less time conducting research and more time making decisions around how to design great digital products. This kind of testing has become an essential, integral, and strategic part of agile development, or the modern way to design and build software.

As Wikipedia describes it, the agile approach "advocates adaptive planning, evolutionary development, early delivery, and continual improvement, and it encourages flexible responses to change." Since digital products are "alive," so to speak, and constantly evolving, this is the kind of development process that is necessary to developing an effective digital presence. Automation makes it possible to scale and reiterate UX testing with real end users frequently—sometimes even daily—without breaking the bank. It makes it possible to test different approaches to or multiple aspects of an interface simultaneously, saving time.

In upcoming chapters, I'll lay out exactly how this kind of UX research works, how to implement it, and what that implementation will require.

─────────── **KEY TAKEAWAYS** ───────────

▶ Everybody wants a great UX for their digital presence. The big challenge, and what prevents a lot of companies from achieving this, is that it's actually very hard.

▶ Companies that responded to the new importance of a great UX, and made the necessary investment in it, prospered even during the pandemic, and they will continue to prosper well into the future—because this *is* the wave of the future; it's what's expected by consumers.

▶ "The twentieth century marketing perspective of 'making people want things' has transitioned to a twenty-first century approach of 'making things people want,' and design—with its focus on users—is the route through which brands will either succeed or fail."

▶ Companies need to know how to organize themselves so they can be effective and efficient in building a great digital experience, and that includes giving a design leader a seat at the top table.

▶ To provide a great digital experience for your users, you need to do regular, well-designed, thorough user experience research and testing, and with automation, companies can conduct UX research studies much more efficiently and cost effectively.

CHAPTER 4

So Much Data!

We are drowning in information but starved for knowledge.
—JOHN NAISBITT, SOCIAL RESEARCHER

Y ou can't manage what you can't measure. Back in the late 1990s, when digital businesses started taking off, and companies realized that they could collect information on their customers and their business activities, they also realized that they needed analytics systems to understand that information—to understand traffic patterns and number of visitors on their websites, product adoption patterns, the success of marketing campaigns, and so on. And everything was carefully monitored and tracked, because it was all digital.

And unlike other mediums, such as TV or radio, gathering all of this data from your digital properties—and a lot more—has just gotten easier as the digital age has progressed. All visitor activity is trackable. Customer relationship management (CRM) systems like Salesforce allow companies to gather data about customers and potential customers. Traffic analytics solutions such as Google Analytics make it simple to monitor what's going on—a visitor abandoning a shopping cart, for instance, or not accessing certain pages that you want them to access. But many websites and products have become so big and complex that data-gathering apps produce a mountain of data for companies to deal with. You've got data coming in from multiple channels and multiple devices about multiple products and offline and online activities. It can be a nightmare! There is so much data available now that we even have a term for the result: data overload.

The fundamental problem of data overload is that too much of the data is not useful. Here are three different problems many organizations face today:

- The data may not be useful, because we haven't been clear about what we want to measure and the best way to do so ahead of time.

- We decide to "measure everything," because it's "easy" to do so, but then we have way too much data.

- Having all that data is overwhelming and makes the job of processing it hard.

And to make things even more challenging on top of this data overload issue, traffic analytics systems only provide you a partial view of your digital business, giving you data related to what has occurred (such as pages visited or abandoned shopping carts), but not the reasons *why* it has occurred. To collect this, you need a very different approach, methodology, knowledge, and tools. To understand the why behind the what, you need user research.

Why User Research Data Is Worth So Much

So, you might ask, why would you want to add *even more* data to this stream by doing user research? Why would you want to add another layer of data? The reason is that the "cold data" you get about user activity via standard analytics—the number of users that visit pages, how long they stay on those pages and on the site, where they drop out, etc.—has to be complemented by what I call "warm data," experiential data that delivers the *why* and the *how* of user activity. It's only the combination of these two types of data that is ultimately going to provide you with actionable insights needed to manage your digital property.

For example, say you've got a shopping site where people are searching your products. The cold data shows you that the product pages are popular. You know how many people were on those pages, how much time they spent there, and what they bought. What you don't know is *why* they were there, why they did what they did while they were there, and *how* they felt about the experience. And that's what UX research delivers: the additional warm, behavioral, qualitative and quantitative data that tells you the why and how.

Because with user research you're actually observing users interacting with your product and directly asking them for their feedback, you get deeper insights into that behavior—into why they're spending so much time on given pages and what they're looking for there and if they've enjoyed the shopping experience. You'll discover if they're looking at product pictures or product descriptions or both, if they feel that the pictures and product descriptions are good enough to help them make a decision to buy, if they care about what other people have to say about your products via reviews, and if they want to be able to click the product pictures to make them bigger. This kind of task-based behavioral and attitudinal information leads to actionable insights that most cold data doesn't deliver.

A lot of companies today are understanding this, and so they're gathering a combination of cold and warm data—a multimethod or mixed-method approach to research and analytics. However, a lot of companies are not there yet. They may have a sophisticated analytics strategy to understand *what* is happening, but they don't have a mature user research strategy that will tell them *why* and *how* things are happening. So they're flying half-blind. Analytics is passive—a one-way street of data gathering. Analytics is typically backward looking (rearview mirror), only flagging up issues after they're live and impacting real customers. User research, while it can make sense of postlive analytics, is like looking out the front windshield—understanding potential risks for your digital product or property on the road ahead—because it can be conducted on a prototype of your digital product before you even launch it to all your customers. User research is a dialogue between you and your customers and potential customers.

In a *UX Collective* article in 2019, product manager, researcher, and writer Triceara J. Heydt described a situation where the combination of cold and warm data provided important insight into customer behavior for the food-delivery company Epicured. The company had been working on the basis of this customer persona: "A female, between the ages of 35 and 54, who does not use a mobile device to access their website."[19] Because of this, they had not invested in a mobile site.

Heydt's company decided to run a combination of user research studies and traffic analysis. Then they ran one-on-one interviews with a handful of Epicured customers. Through the interviews, they were able to pinpoint exactly where and why users got frustrated in their use of Epicured's website (the lack of availability of a mobile site and confusion on the ordering/account page). Next, Heydt turned to Google Analytics to see what she could learn:

> At first, we weren't quite sure how this data would help us. Then, late one night, I was exploring the analytics page and

---

19   Triceara J. Heydt, "User Research & Google Analytics—A UX Case Study," *UX Collective*, February 9, 2019, https://uxdesign.cc/a-tool-has-a-prescribed-use-but-it-can-be-used-for-many-purposes-a2a562cd7e34].

saw something that was interesting to say the least. Analyzing their revenue and current customers, I saw that more than half of their users were between the ages of 25 and 34; they represent Epicured's single largest user age group. I also saw that most of Epicured's revenue came from users ages 25 to 44. I excitedly sent screenshots of this data to my teammates. Intrigued, I continued to explore the analytics page even further. The most shocking revelation? 66% of Epicured's users are female, but male customers nearly matched the spending of female customers.

With this combination of warm and cold data, Epicured was able to refine its user profile and therefore how it marketed itself, and they invested in a mobile website to satisfy the customers they *actually had*, not the ones they'd *thought they had*.

Another example is from PayPal. Over a decade ago, the user research team at PayPal observed, in a usability test, that users were struggling with entering phone numbers (ten digits) because back then the field did not accept dashes (–) or brackets (()), and different people typed phone numbers in different ways. The field provided an error message and the right way of typing phone numbers, so it was not a fatal mistake but an annoyance that caused a moment of frustration. That's the warm data that generates empathy for the end user. Armed with this insight, the team quickly dove deeper in analytics to "size" the issue, to see how many users on the live site encountered that error message. Also, the conversion rate difference between the people that encountered that error versus users that did not in a given time period. That way they could quantify, come up with a dollar figure, to push the fix of being flexible in accepting phone numbers, per country, in varying formats.

Via analytics they would have known that there is a potential issue, but via direct observation of a user encountering the problem, they knew what to look for in the large quantities of analytics data. Sometimes the cold analytics data points to an area to investigate further, and warm UX research observational data tells you the *why*. Other times, warm observational data from UX research helps to look further, deep dive, and quantify using cold analytics data, as in this example.

The last example is from Reckitt (formerly Reckitt Benckiser), which used warm data generated from the user research platform at my company (UserZoom) to tell them the why behind customer behavior leading to a 20 percent increase in conversions.

Like many consumer packaged goods (CPG) companies, Reckitt's e-commerce sales to consumers were conducted on third-party sites, such as grocery sites and marketplaces, not websites they owned. This meant the cold data they could access was very limited. So they leveraged user research to generate warm data of online assets (like product imagery and descriptions) to understand how to make their online product pages on third-party sites more compelling.

Armed with the *why* from user research, they, in the words of their e-commerce manager, "were able to change the elements of our e-commerce content that were most closely linked with conversion rates, ultimately leading to an increase in sales."

Read more about this case study at https://www.userzoom.com/our-customers/reckitt-benckiser/.

If you want to be a successful digital experience company today—and into the future—you're going to *have to* combine your analytics and operational data with user experience data. You're going to need those insights into the why and the how to complement each other—and help you more thoroughly understand what is happening with your products and services. This combination will provide you with deeper insights, give you the whole picture that will help you make wise decisions about the design and features of your products and services.

Why Companies Resist UX Research— and Why They Shouldn't

Yes, doing both analytics and UX research requires an investment of time and money, but what this delivers is so valuable in the digital age that it cannot be neglected. One reason companies have resisted UX research is that analytics became so automated that it was cheap and relatively easy to do. UX research, on the other hand, tended to be slow, costly, and time consuming—just plain hard to do. It took a lot more effort. So they just didn't do it. They said, "Oh, I have so much data already" or "It's too expensive" or "I already know what my customers want." They just launched products and services and if they worked, great. If they didn't, they fixed them. But if you think UX research is expensive, think about how expensive *that* process is: fixing and rereleasing something.

And that's why successful digital companies have never operated that way. They don't just throw products and services out there to see if they sink or swim. They anticipate the market, test out their features and designs early on to see if they're going down the right path—the path to popularity, success, and profitability.

And the good news is you can afford to operate that way now too. UX research is not free and not without effort, but what used to be a manual, in-person process that was extremely expensive is now a lot more automated and simpler. As mentioned in the previous chapter, automation has made it much easier to do *both* analytics and user research, to gather both cold and warm data, and to combine the two and deepen your knowledge of what your customers and potential customers want.

Automated UX research now delivers, swiftly and cost effectively, information that makes products function better and sell better. It's that simple. In the past, if you wanted to do user interviews or usability testing, it would take you easily two weeks, three weeks, sometimes a month. Now you can use software and the Internet to invite people remotely to participate in a study, and you can get valuable feedback in a matter of hours!

This is why it's now possible to integrate UX research into the agile approach to development, which I described briefly in the previous chapter. You can get the results quickly and act on them quickly—within a short agile development "sprint." The results of UX research are not delivered in long, labored reports; they're delivered in "nuggets"—brief, swift observations of the user experience that can be acted on quickly to improve a product.

Automated UX research now delivers, swiftly and cost effectively, information that makes products function better and sell better. It's that simple.

For instance, a nugget could be a few video clips that show comments from users about the illustration on a page, and that video could represent a UX survey where a hundred users reacted negatively to the illustration. And these nuggets can be tagged and easily made available to the whole development team as reference points for making changes. As UX expert Tomer Sharon has put it, "Imagine 1,000 such nuggets. Properly tagged, well defined, easily searched and found. Beats any report."[20]

---

20   Tomer Sharon, "The Atomic Unit of Research Insight," Medium, September 8, 2016, https://medium.com/@tsharon/the-atomic-unit-of-a-research-insight-7bf13ec8fabe.

This is the kind of so-called democratization of insights that's going on in digital companies now—and in some of them since their inception. Typically a user researcher will conduct the study and of course collect the data from test participants. But then product managers are going to want to access the data as well to make decisions. Designers are going to want to access the data. Sometimes even company executive leaders are going to want to access it. When you're a digital experience company, you collaborate among teams. So data and insights flow from one part of the company to another; they're shared openly via the cloud so that everyone stays focused on user needs and wants.

This open, iterative approach enables you to take a minimal viable product (MVP) and put it in front of users, get a response to it, and quickly improve it—and it enables as many iterations of this process as you need. Fixing problems in a product during this kind of process is much less expensive than it was in the old "waterfall" approach to development, where the product was much further along before it was tested, making changes more difficult and expensive.

Another way to "test tentatively," even more so than releasing an MVP, is to build a simple prototype and test that. This gives you even earlier insights that could be very helpful in informing the product and experience, even before committing to code at all (even for MVP).

Company organization can affect how much influence UX testing and expertise can have on development. Dropbox is a company that has found integrating UX research into their development process highly valuable—so much so that UX research experts are now part of every development team—as Christopher Nash, a senior design researcher there, related:

> As soon as the team was big enough, we began to special-
> ize, embedding researchers in product areas and product

teams. The embedded model came with significant benefits. Researchers built ongoing relationships with their teams, developing mutual trust and respect, and they were able to develop deep domain knowledge. We didn't have to burn time ramping up on a new product area for every project. Being embedded with teams also meant that we were in the room for road mapping, planning, and strategy conversations. We were able to advocate for users on a daily basis and reiterate the lessons we'd learned from previous research.

As product teams learned the value of research, they began to rely on researchers more and more to inform product decisions and, eventually, for innovation and strategy. Now they wanted to put everything in front of users.[21]

As I said earlier, there can be so much data that it's overwhelming. But if you come to understand how valuable and cost effective user experience data has become, you'll realize that there is no excuse for *not* gathering that data to complement your analytics data. The end user is always at the center of the agile development process, and automated UX testing truly analyzes the end user *experience*, providing feedback that can be rapidly acted on during product development.

──────── **KEY TAKEAWAYS** ────────

► The fundamental problem of data overload is that too much data is not useful. It leads to data fatigue, because too much data is very difficult to manage; it's difficult to figure out what it means and make it actionable.

---

21 "Scaling Research at Dropbox," *UX Collective*, September 27, 2020, https://uxdesign.cc/scaling-research-at-dropbox-179126f3e45a.

► The cold data you get about user activity via standard analytics has to be complemented by warm data, experiential data that delivers the why and how of user activity. It's only the combination of these two types of data that is actionable.

► This data combination will provide you with deeper insights, give you the whole picture that will help you make wise decisions about the design and features of your products and services.

► Doing both traffic and usage analytics and UX research requires an investment of time and money, but what it delivers is so valuable in the digital age that it cannot be neglected— and the automation of UX research has made it much more affordable.

► It is now possible to integrate UX research into the agile approach to development, allowing you to get results quickly and act on them quickly—within a short agile development "sprint."

CHAPTER 5

Test It, Get It Right: The Importance of User Experience Research

Testing leads to failure, and failure leads to understanding.
—BURT RUTAN, AEROSPACE ENGINEER

There is a UX maturity curve (see the UX Maturity Model below), and it is the companies that are further along on this curve that are the most successful digital experience companies. Wherever your company is on that curve, you need to understand that you *are* a digital experience company, that you are on a digital transformation journey—because, if you're not, you're going the way of the dinosaurs.

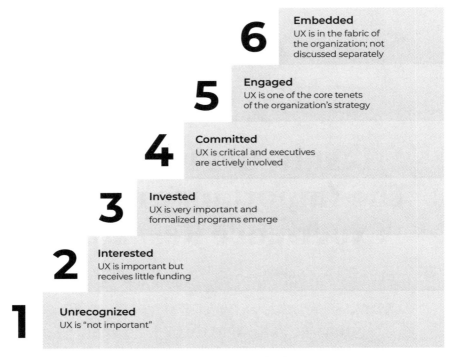

6 **Embedded**
UX is in the fabric of
the organization; not
discussed separately

5 **Engaged**
UX is one of the core tenets
of the organization's strategy

4 **Committed**
UX is critical and executives
are actively involved

3 **Invested**
UX is very important and
formalized programs emerge

2 **Interested**
UX is important but
receives little funding

1 **Unrecognized**
UX is "not important"

The User Experience Maturity Model, by Renato Feijó
Source: https://medium.com/@erangatl/user-experience-maturity-model-364ef36a6c67

Just saying that you want to offer great digital experiences is one thing, but acting on that intention—putting your money where your mouth is, as the saying goes—is an entirely different thing. You need to understand where your company falls on the UX Maturity Model and move the needle.

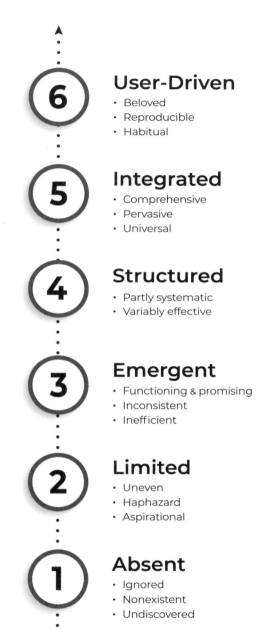

The 6 Levels of UX Maturity, by Kara Pernice, Sarah Gibbons, Kate Moran, and Kathryn Whitenton
Source: https://www.nngroup.com/articles/ux-maturity-model/

At UserZoom we have developed a maturity model that focuses on UX research and evaluates UX capability across five areas: people, execution, operations, impact, and C-suite. You'll need to lead across all of these areas in order to offer great digital experiences.

	PEOPLE	EXECUTION	OPERATIONS	IMPACT	C-SUITE
Level 4 "LEADING"	Senior research leadership roles	Fully integrated and consistent user research across all product teams	Full road map, robust process, research ops function	Links UX to business KPIs, UX research informs overall product strategy	Executives are leaned in. UX research has a seat at the table.
Level 3 "DEVELOPED"	Dedicated research function with hierarchy in place	Research across product development life cycle, beginnings of benchmark	Research best practices, some road mapping	Measuring to inform UX impact on KPIs	Good budget availability
Level 2 "PROGRESSING"	Some expertise but low manpower	UX researcher mainly on large projects	No consistent process, more individual reliance	Help inform design decisions	Tends not to reach exec
Level 1 "STARTER"	No dedicated research team	Mainly qualitative/ guerrilla testing	Insight sits with individuals	Done to validate or find out what customers like or don't like	Little to no exec buy in or budget

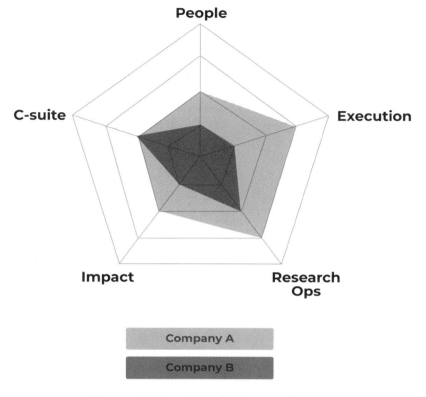

UX Research Maturity Model Summary, UserZoom

The five capability areas are as follows:

1. People: Who conducts research in the organization and how well equipped are they to succeed?

2. Execution: How does the organization run UX research?

3. Operations: What level of rigor or standards does the organization have in place for UX research?

4. Impact: What is the purpose of the research, and what is its impact on the organization?

5. C-suite: What relationship exists between UX research and the organization's senior leadership?

Do you understand what a great digital presence is all about? Are you acting on the development of that digital presence? Do you have the right resources? Are you making the necessary investment to make it happen? Do you have a UX research operations team in place? The point of the UX maturity models is to show how companies increasingly include user research into their processes as they become more mature.

You need to devise a product UX design and research road map, and this entails a new way of designing and building software. The end user must be part of the process—the center of the process, in fact—for everyone on the product development team, whether it's a designer or a product manager or a software developer or a marketer. You need to do UX research and testing throughout the product development cycle.

This approach dovetails with the wildly popular agile approach to product development. On one hand, there is really nothing in the agile development process that spells out user research (you have to essentially insert it into agile if you want to have a user-centered design process that works with agile). However, agile does provide the opportunity to leverage user research insights at various points, such as in specific agile sprints. But it doesn't happen automatically, since many companies practice agile but are not UX mature. The agile approach starts with a requirements and discovery phase and then moves through design, develop, test, display, and review stages—and it does this iteratively. You should be running user research during all of these phases, and with the lower cost of digital UX research and testing, you can afford to do that.

There are two situations with digital product development: either you're creating a new product from scratch or you have an existing product that you want to optimize. In both cases, you should start with user research. For instance, a competitive benchmark analysis, a point of reference that establishes where you are today, is a great way to start. So if you're creating a new product, you need to establish what's out there now, what the level of need is for a new product, and what competitors might be providing in this area, if anything. Then with persona analysis, you will discover the needs of potential target users in the market you want to enter. So there's a lot of discovery research that needs to be done to help you understand the market and the opportunity. It's very similar to what you would do as an entrepreneur at a start-up.

If you're optimizing an existing product, through a benchmark usability study you'll also need to discover the pain points of your current users in the current version of the product and what alternatives might be in the market, so you can design an improved product that better answers current users' needs and attracts new users.

In order to find out what you need to know to produce a new or improved product experience, you'll develop a concept, wireframe, prototype—something simple and, as we describe it, "low fidelity"—that potential users can interact with and respond to. This is how designers and developers figure out things such as where to put different elements on the limited real estate of a screen so users can find them, how to make sure that users have a clear path to achieving what they need to achieve. You might even test different versions of a product, what we call A/B design testing.

Here's a challenge in this particular stage: the people trying to develop or improve a product get too close to it; it's exceedingly difficult for them to stand back and imagine someone encountering the product for the first time. And that's what UX research and usability testing provides: that fresh, objective perspective and feedback. And this testing needs to be iterative. It needs to happen early and often at each phase of development—not to mention before actual coding or development even starts at the concept stage. Working this way is much more likely to lead to success, because it reduces risk by uncovering and addressing UX problems that are less expensive to address than when discovered later.

Gartner analyst Jane-Anne Mennella concludes that

> test and learn is more than a process; it's an ethos successful companies embody to create powerful products, campaigns and customer experiences. Loyalty and customer relationship leaders who build a test-and-learn culture can reduce cost while increasing customer acquisition and retention.[22]

The Focus of UX Research and Usability Testing

UX research and usability testing are both focused on the quality of the experience users are having, if they're easily able to do specific tasks (effectiveness or success ratio), and how they go about achieving those tasks (efficiency ratio). You ask users to complete a task, and you observe how they do it, and they optionally you ask questions about why they did it the way they did and if they found it easy, convenient (and even fun when it applies), or confusing and tedious. Through this process, you learn the how and the why of user interaction with your product, as well as how users feel about the experience. This is why it's very important to test early and often—every week or every other week—as you move forward in your design and development process.

You may start out testing on basic mockups and low-fidelity wireframes, but eventually you'll have a fully interactive product, a

---

22   "Build a Test-and-Learn Culture to Drive Digital Transformation," Gartner, October 26, 2020.

high-fidelity prototype. In research this is called a stimulus. The more basic the stimulus is, the more conversational the study is. As the stimulus becomes more advanced, the more behavioral your focus can be. You let users do everything on their own, go through the product's full workflow, because at that point the product's almost built and can be fully explored, and so the research should be all about observing (and less about questioning). After a certain amount of such testing, you'll have the confidence to go live with the product. It may not be perfect, but through your use of UX research and usability testing, you greatly reduce the risk of releasing a product with serious limitations or problems.

These are the kinds of activities that make up UX research and testing:[23]

TOP UX RESEARCH METHODS	
DISCOVER	• Field study • Diary study • User interview • Stakeholder interview • Requirements and constraints gathering
EXPLORE	• Competitive analysis • Design review • Persona building • Task analysis • Journey mapping • Prototype feedback and testing (clickable or paper prototypes) • Writing of user stories • Card sorting
TEST	• Qualitative usability testing (in-person or remote) • Benchmark testing • Accessibility evaluation
LISTEN	• Survey • Analytics review • Search log analysis • Usability bug review • Frequently asked questions (FAQ) review

23   "UX Research Cheat Sheet," Nielson Normal Group, https://www.nngroup.com/articles/ux-research-cheat-sheet/.

What kind of metrics do you derive from this kind of testing? At UserZoom, we collect metrics on both user behavior and user attitude.

BEHAVIOR (WHAT THEY DO)

In the user research world, it's critical to understand what people are doing and how they are using your products. Task-based usability testing is a standard method to gather this information across the industry. We don't mean just "in-lab" think-out-loud studies but also remote unmoderated studies, which access larger sample sizes in an efficient way.

Typical metrics you could capture include these task-level behavioral measurements:

- **Page Views**—Some combination of clicks, taps, number of screens and steps

- **Problems and Frustrations**—Number of unique problems identified and/or number (or percentage) of participants that encounter a certain problem

- **Task Success**—Percentage of users, given a set of realistic tasks with a clear definition of task success, who succeed at the task

- **Task Time**—Time spent to complete a given task

And for sites that include direct sales, this can be combined with cold data such as the following:

- **Abandonment Rate**—The ratio of the number of abandoned shopping carts to the number of initiated transactions

- **Average Order Value**—Total revenue divided by number of checkouts

- **Conversions**—Number of sales divided by the number of visits

ATTITUDE (WHAT THEY SAY)

These metrics capture how users feel; what they say before, during, or after using a product; and how this affects brand perception. To measure this, you might want to capture these attitudinal metrics:

- **Net Promoter Score (NPS)**—Measures loyalty based on one direct question: How likely is it that you would recommend this company/product/service/experience to a friend or colleague?

- **Standardized User Experience Percentile Rank Question-naire (SUPR-Q)**—Eight-item questionnaire for measuring the quality of the website user experience, providing measures of usability, credibility, loyalty, and appearance.

- **System Usability Scale (SUS)**—Score derived from a short questionnaire that ascribes a quantitative value to qualitative opinions.

- **Task Performance Indicator (TPI)**—User is presented with a task question, and once they have completed the task, they answer the question and then indicate how confident they are in their answer.

THE SYSTEM USABILITY SCALE STANDARD VERSION		STRONGLY DISAGREE				STRONGLY AGREE
1	I think that I would like to use this system frequently.	1	2	3	4	5
2	I found the system unnecessarily complex.	O	O	O	O	O
3	I thought the system was easy to use.	O	O	O	O	O
4	I think that I would need the support of a technical person to be able to use this system.	O	O	O	O	O
5	I found the various functions in this system were well integrated.	O	O	O	O	O
6	I thought there was too much inconsistency in this system.	O	O	O	O	O
7	I would imagine that most people would learn to use this system very quickly.	O	O	O	O	O
8	I found the system very awkward to use.	O	O	O	O	O
9	I felt very confident using the system.	O	O	O	O	O
10	I needed to learn a lot of things before I could get going with this system.	O	O	O	O	O

System Usability Scale (SUS)

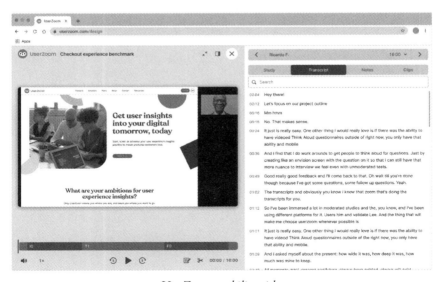

UserZoom usability video

UserZoom heatmap results

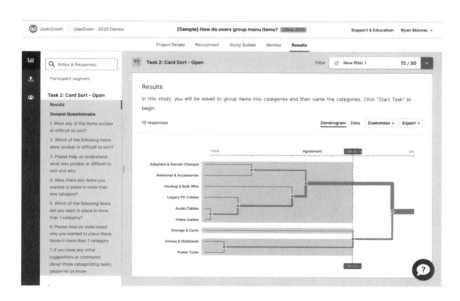

UserZoom card-sorting results

UserZoom also has its own single UX metric score, called the QXscore—a "quality of experience" score that combines various measurements, collecting both behavioral data (such as task success, task time, page views) and attitudinal data (such as ease of use, trust, and appearance).

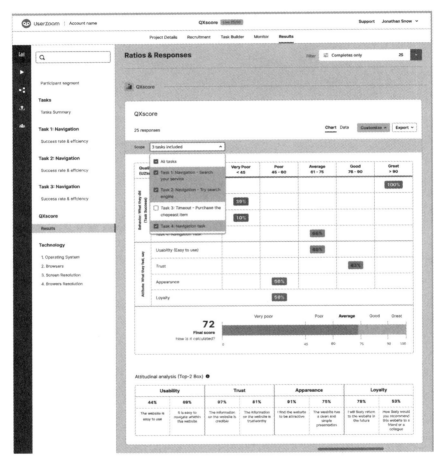

UserZoom QXscore

This may seem like a lot of data to gather, and as I said earlier in the book, this type of research used to be complicated, time consuming, tedious, and expensive, but it has now been automated using sophisticated software. Automation allows you to collect and store and control user data, as well as share it across teams for faster, leaner, more cost-effective UX development. This has enabled companies to be much more frequent, efficient, and cost effective in their use of research and testing—to the point where there's no excuse not to do it, especially when your company's future is likely to depend on it.

Quantitative data gathering and qualitative data gathering are two different kinds of research projects. Qualitative research is something you mostly do during the early stages of product development, because you're just trying get a feel for how things are working and whether they're working the way you want them to be working before you nail down features. And then you do quantitative research to make sure that a large number of users can handle using the product and are happy about the experience.

Here is a graphic that details the types of quantitative and qualitative research methods:

A Landscape of User Research Methods

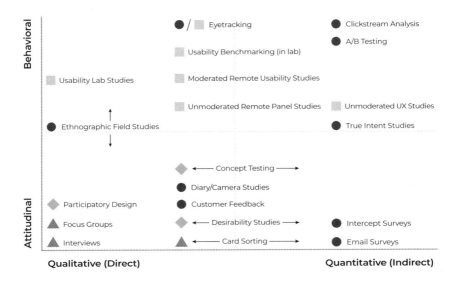

Key for context of product use during data collection

● Natural use of product   ▲ Decontextualized / not using product

▨ Scripted (often lab-based) use of product   ◆ Combination / hybrid

Source: Christian Rohrer, https://www.nngroup.com/articles/
which-ux-research-methods/

Let's highlight a few of the key UX research methods that are important to conduct:

CONCEPT TESTING

Test often; fail fast; get it right. Well, the best way to do that is to rapidly collect user feedback on early concepts, sketches, wireframes, or prototypes. This can be a simple, small-sample-size, qualitative click test, a five-second test, or a think-out-loud usability study to glean insights. These can be followed up with larger-sample-size quantitative usability research to get to be relatively confident that the ideas you have and the designs and solutions you have will strike a chord with your target audience.

ETHNOGRAPHIC FIELD STUDIES

These days we would call them discovering needs and opportunities via remote interviews at the beginning of the project. The aim is not just to gather information on how people behave and interact but also how their location, environment, and other contexts affect their day-to-day lives. The intent is to spend some quality time building empathy of the target market, a deeper understanding of the challenges and goals of the end users. These tend to be qualitative in nature to get to warm insights and stories from real people.

SURVEYS

Surveys are commonly known as a way to collect feedback. Users can be intercepted directly from your website or app. Typically, surveys are quantitative because you are asking rating scale–type questions, and the goal is to get statistically significant sample sizes to ensure your decisions are backed by the numbers. You can, however, get qualitative insights from asking open-ended questions to get information that wouldn't necessarily fit into a typical rating scale.

USABILITY STUDIES (IN-LAB, REMOTE MODERATED, OR UNMODERATED)

A usability study is the most-used research method for UX testing. It can be conducted live (moderated), typically one on one with a moderator and a participant, or conducted asynchronously (unmoderated), where a research study is built, and participants verbalize their thoughts as they go through the experience on their own time. Both are valuable in understanding if the end users can perform tasks and provide feedback. The key is observing what users can and cannot do, how the designs fit their mental model as well as their attitudes (likes, dislikes, preferences). Usability studies tend to be smaller sample sizes (five to ten participants) because the intent is to get to the warm insights. Typically, usability studies are followed by a large-sample, unmoderated benchmarking study or surveys to get to higher confidence—lower margin of error.

USABILITY BENCHMARKING

Usability benchmarking allows you to measure your digital product's baseline performance and how changes are affecting the UX needle over time. Typical benchmark studies are either longitudinal, in which you continually measure your own products over time, or competitive, in which you measure your product's performance against others.

With benchmarking, you can send your participants off to carry out the same identical tasks on a variety of websites (including your own) in order to determine the following:

- How your site performs relative to your competitors

- Your usability standing, feature set, and more within your industry

- Others' success and failures—what works or does not for your competitors

- Industry best-in-class examples to emulate

- Benchmark with other industries

In order to score the sites, you can combine various measurements, collecting both behavioral data (such as task success, task time, page views) and attitudinal data (such as ease of use, trust, and appearance). QXscore, covered previously, combines behavioral data and attitudinal data.

CARD SORTING

In a card sort, participants are presented with a list of items (for example, all the products featured in an online supermarket) and asked to group them in a way that makes the most logical sense to them. Depending on the type of card sort, participants can also choose names for the groups they've put together, forming the potential categories and subcategories of a website.

A/B TESTING

A/B testing, like the name suggests, is the ability to test two or more design solutions to determine the winning design that optimizes given key performance indicators (KPIs). A/B testing can be performed during early design stages to determine best design options between design A or design B (or A/B/C/D). The most common use of A/B testing is live site, throttling a percentage of users to go through design version A and the rest through version B and over time monitoring which one leads to better KPIs (conversion rate, for example).

The Competitive Landscape

Having covered the methods landscape in the previous section, I also want to help you understand more about the companies that compete in this industry. As a CEO, I get to talk to a lot of people, such as UserZoom's customers and users, prospects, partners, analysts (like Gartner and Forrester), and employees, as well as investors. Especially among leaders, more so than with actual practitioners, I very often get asked to explain the value of user research as well as what it is that we do at UserZoom compared to other companies. One reason this happens often is that the market is relatively young, and many software companies have only been in business for less than ten years—often less than five years. Also, there are subtle differences between many of them, and so many people who are not directly involved in the market have questions about what each company focuses on.

The digital experience research and analytics market, as I define the category, has experienced phenomenal growth in the last five years. I expect it to continue growing due to a great extent to the pandemic and the greater focus on digital. As the number of digital transformation projects takes off, so does the number of companies supporting the path to digital. Also, as I've covered in the book thus far, the need to be truly customer centric and deeply understand the end user and customer experience is key to success.

So in sum, the market is getting big. Just in the last couple of years, we've seen a great volume of capital investment or M&A (mergers and acquisitions) activity in the space. Here are just some examples of recent transactions to prove the point:

- In 2021, Contentsquare raised a $500 million round at a $2.8 billion valuation and then purchased a popular analytics company called Hotjar.

- Andreesen Horowitz, one of the most prestigious investors in Silicon Valley, invested $50 million in Figma, a design software company that's worth $1 billion as of August 2021.

- Qualtrics, an experience management company, was acquired by German software giant SAP for $8 billion back in late 2018. Then this year, 2021, the company acquired Clarabridge for $1.1 billion.

- The Amplitude IPO.

- And one close to me, of course: in 2020, right during the pandemic, UserZoom raised $100 million from Owl Rock at a near half-billion-dollar valuation.

The reason there are so many transactions is obvious: the market is growing, the demand for digital experience insights is growing, and companies are positioning themselves to grab more land and win more customers.

When it comes to describing the digital experience research and analytics category and subcategories, as well as the different types of companies providing solutions in the market, I think about two ways to describe the landscape:

A) PRODUCT DESIGN AND DEVELOPMENT CYCLE

The product development life cycle and process description allow for a focus on the stages when a vendor is used and adopted by the end users within the company that buys that vendor's product. Figure 1 below represents a typical software product development cycle, with six main stages.

Figure 1
Source: Relevant, 7 Steps of Effective Software Product Development Life Cycle,
https://relevant.software/blog/7-steps-for-effective-software-product-development/.

Figure 2 below represents a user-centered design (UCD) process and stages with UX research substages included. It's very related to the software development shown above, with the initial stage being the light-blue "user-focused product decisions" stage and the "consideration" substage. I like this chart because it includes three main stages, each with its three substages, specifically focused on research and analytics (versus the broader figure above).

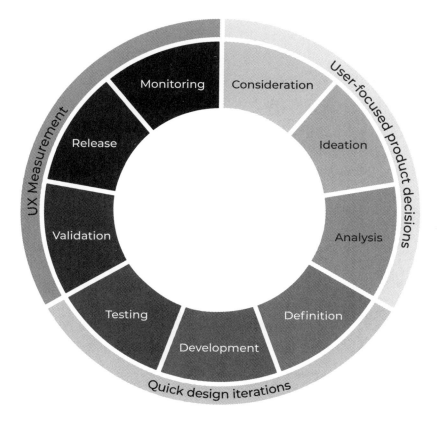

Figure 2

Here are examples of UX and CX research vendors that focus on each specific stage. Please note that these are just a few examples; there are many more. See many of them in figure 3 below. This is meant to generally explain the focus and types of vendors in the landscape.

User-focused product decisions stage:

- dscout

- Indeemo

- UserZoom

Quick design iterations stage:

- Optimal Workshop

- Lookback

- Userlytics

- Maze

- UsabilityHub

- UserTesting

- UserZoom

UX / CX measurement:

- Qualtrics

- Momentive (formerly SurveyMonkey)

- Medallia

- Sauce Labs

- Pendo

- UserTesting

- UserZoom

B) ACTIVE VERSUS PASSIVE INSIGHTS

Another way to look at the landscape is through the active-versus-passive lens. I like the work done by the team at Userinterviews.com (a partner of UserZoom's, by the way) to come up with the map shown on figure 3 below, from 2020. They divided the market into five main subcategories:

1. Active Research

2. ResearchOps

3. Insight Management

4. Passive Insights

5. Design

Note that while the model created may not be 100 percent accurate, it's really difficult to put this together, because there is quite a bit of overlap between some of these vendors. But ultimately, the main goal of this chart is to offer a general overview of the landscape, and I believe they've done a very good job with it.

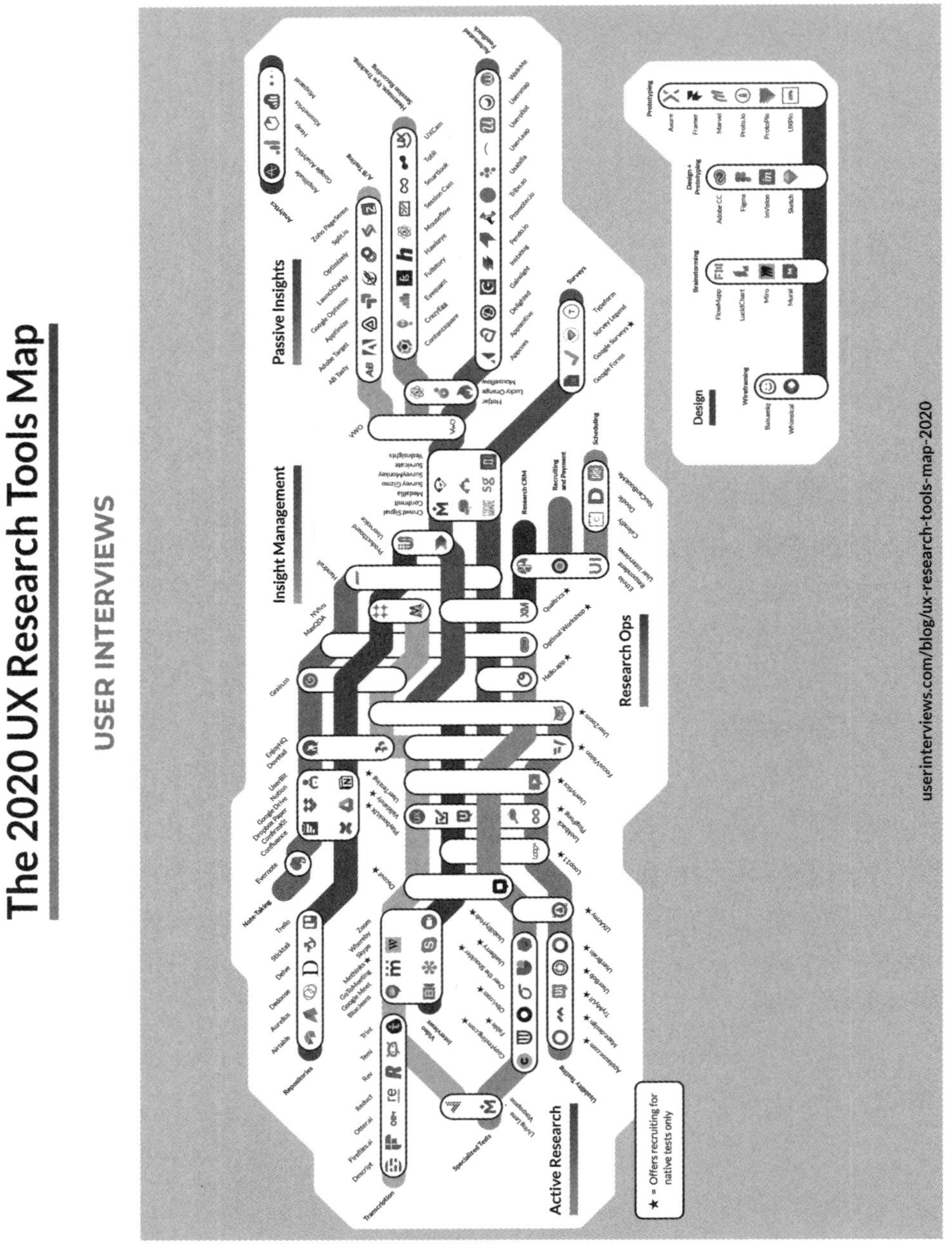

The 2020 UX Research Tools Map

USER INTERVIEWS

Figure 3
Source: Userinterviews.com, https://www.userinterviews.com/blog/
ux-research-tools-map-2020.

MIXED METHODS AND RESEARCH TRIANGULATION

So which of these methods should teams use to become successful digital experience companies? Actually, the best choice is to adopt a multimethod (also known as mixed-method) approach. As Nielsen Norman Group suggests in the article "Triangulation: Get Better Research Results by Using Multiple UX Methods," diversifying user research methods ensures more reliable, valid results by considering multiple ways of collecting and interpreting data.

So what does triangulation actually mean? As the article puts it, "All research methods are limited in some way. But the solution to overcoming these limitations is not to throw up our hands and quit doing research. Instead, the best approach is to use multiple research methods, so the limitations of one method are mitigated by data from another source. This approach of applying multiple research techniques is called triangulation."[24]

Triangulation can take many forms; two examples of how you could triangulate UX research are shown in figure 4 below. Left: Triangulate by using multiple methods to study the same activity, such as quantitative research, qualitative research, and expert review. Right: Triangulate by analyzing several different metrics related to the same activity, such as satisfaction ratings, time spent, and revenue volume.

---

24 Kathryn Whitenton, "Triangulation: Get Better Research Results by Using Multiple UX Methods," Nielsen Norman Group, February 21, 2021, https://www.nngroup.com/articles/triangulation-better-research-results-using-multiple-ux-methods/.

Figure 4
Source: Nielsen Norman Group, https://www.nngroup.com/articles/
triangulation-better-research-results-using-multiple-ux-methods/.

Some examples of research triangulation follow:

- Satisfaction metrics decline → you check revenue and time spent to see if they also changed.

- A quantitative usability test indicates low subscription form success rates → you do a qualitative study to understand what features are problematic.

- Sales team reports that users think the software is hard to use → you do a usability study to observe problems.

- Analytics data indicates a feature has high error rates → you check customer support records to determine if problems are reported with this feature.

- Interviews suggest a surprising purchase motivation → you do a survey to assess the frequency of that motivation.

- One researcher notes several themes in interview transcripts → another researcher does a separate theme analysis to check if she finds the same themes.

The Importance of Research Ops

There are more UX research projects now than ever before. At UserZoom, for instance, in the last three and a half years we've experienced a 900 percent increase in the number of studies and a 470 percent increase in the number of participants who took part in UX studies (see figure 5 below). UserZoom's customers, mostly UX researchers and designers, are running studies on a continuous basis (weekly or biweekly), often multiple studies concurrently (or in parallel), to achieve efficiency. In 2020 alone, UserZoom's customers conducted over thirty-three thousand studies and over 2.5 million participants completed a study. That's an incredible amount of research!

Total Studies Launched

Studies with three or more completes, first launch date

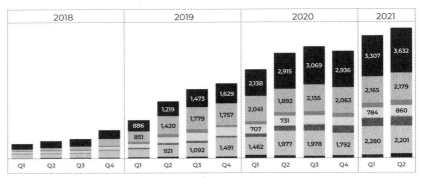

Figure 5

Source: UserZoom Product Management Team: 900 percent increase in the number of studies

But achieving great UX research is not just about adding designer and researcher roles; it's about building a research operations program and team that can execute valuable research consistently and efficiently with the support of the whole company.

As defined by Re+Ops, "ResearchOps is the people, mechanisms, and strategies that set user research in motion. It provides the roles, tools and processes needed to support researchers in delivering and scaling the impact of the craft across an organisation."[25]

---

25 "About," Re+Ops, accessed October 18, 2021, https://researchops.community/about/.

Carrie Boyd of User Interviews writes,

Establishing a research ops team can work wonders for your research practice as a whole. In a large organization, having a team in charge of the facilitation of a research practice is a near necessity to do effective, efficient, and within-budget research.

A research ops function—a person or a team—will help you deliver research and insights effectively and efficiently. ... If the goal of research is to make better decisions through better insights, research ops should ultimately help your business make better decisions to be more successful.[26]

---

26   Carrie Boyd, "Research Ops: What It Is and Why It's So Important," User Interviews, https://www.userinterviews.com/blog/research-ops-what-it-is-and-why-its-so-important.

Boyd goes on to say that you're likely to need research ops to coordinate your UX research when you have eight or more researchers. You can start off with one person in charge of research ops, but the ops team will need to grow as your research team grows, and coordinating all of the research and testing gets more challenging. "In large teams," she says, "things like participant recruitment, asset management, and budget management can be a research ops team member's entire focus. Asking one person to address everything, or trying to address everything while being a full-time researcher, would be like asking someone to have twelve part-time jobs while starting a business. You can do it, but you probably won't be doing everything well …"

Another aspect of research ops is how practice is embedded within the organization. According to Kate Towsey, research ops manager at Atlassian and a thought leader in the space, research operations "provides the infrastructure that helps support and shape how research is seen and done in an organization."[27] Crucially, this is not just about the tools or solutions used within a business but how these in turn shape culture and practice to deliver against these aims. Kate warns against what she calls "candy floss research"—quick, easy, and cheap research optimized for quantity over quality. While a quick fix is sometimes necessary, a culture of quality, robust research is ultimately where mature organizations need to be headed as experience insights become increasingly critical to business success.

The whole point of research ops is to make sure that researchers and designers get the behavioral information they need to define the best digital experience for customers and potential customers. Because user research is a big investment, having it well managed and effective is important to the bottom line.

---

27   "Turbocharge your research practice with Research Ops," UserZoom, webinar, accessed October 18, 2021, https://info.userzoom.com/Research-Ops-Webinar_Confirmation.html.

Also important to the success of UX research is the involvement of C-level executives. Top management needs to be sensitive to what the UX research team is doing. After all, the company is—or should be—investing a good bit of money in this research, and they should be paying attention to whether it's paying off or not, paying attention to the kinds of metrics I discussed above. But UX research won't pay off unless it's part of the company's culture, unless its importance is recognized from top to bottom. It demands a culture change that makes a great digital experience for users a top priority.

It's important for those at the top to hear what the customer is experiencing, because what they're experiencing is perceived as the company's brand—that's just the nature of a digital experience company. It's all about how your products work and how they make your customer feel. It's going to impact your bottom line. So top management needs to understand the user experience and make product decisions based on what those users need and want.

Cristine Cravens, the user research and product design leader at Kroger, has made her company's research scalable by developing a research ops practice that empowers all the designers on her team. With seventy designers, she indicates, it's important that the best practices for this research are widely understood and followed. So they have developed processes and templates that are easily available to anyone and everyone who is doing user research.

Product designers are part of the research ops practice and were part of the effort when the team got together and decided on Kroger's priorities when doing user research. For example, they put a process in place that has researchers review any design study a designer comes up with to ensure the quality of that study. This cooperation between designers and researchers has raised the level of user research results for the company and ensured that its research practice will continually improve.

"The important thing," says Cravens, "is that taking this time to focus on our operations allows us to stay agile and nimble … while we continue to mature our research practice."

KEY TAKEAWAYS

► Just saying that you want to offer great digital experiences is one thing, but you must act on that intention. The end user must be the center of the process for everyone on the product development team—and this requires research.

► If you're creating a new product, you need to establish what's out there now, what the level of need is for a new product, what competitors offer, and what needs potential users have. If you're optimizing an existing product, you need to discover the pain points of your current users and what alternatives might be in the market, so you can design an improved product that answers current users' needs and attracts new users.

► UX research and testing is focused on the quality of the experience users are having, if they're easily able to do specific tasks, and how they go about achieving those tasks. And you need to test both behavior and attitude.

► A good UX research operations department can execute this essential research more efficiently and consistently, but they need the involvement and support of the whole company—especially C-level executives.

CHAPTER 6

Sourcing Participants for Your Research

Working with users from the beginning of a product cycle ensures
that the product is being designed so that users will be satisfied.
—CLARE-MARIE KARAT, KARAT CONSULTING

A s important as *how* you test your product with the end users (or potential users) is determining *which* ones to invite to participate in the test. Real feedback from real people is essential to the success of UX research. The quality of your results is dependent on the quality of the people you test your product with. Quality means that these people fit your target product audience profile as closely as possible. You can't just enlist people randomly. You need to know what kind of people reflect your users or potential users. Input and insights from people who aren't the ones your products and services are aimed at are far less valuable—if they have any value at all—than feedback from well-targeted users.

For example, if your product is aimed at selling houses, you don't want input from people who are not considering buying a house or who are financially incapable of it. If your test participants are all digitally savvy, you won't find out what digitally unsophisticated people will experience. If you're targeting women, and you mostly test with men, the same will be true. If you're Lego, you're targeting young people and their parents, so you're going to want to test with both of those groups—not single people with dogs. If you're Ferrari, you need to recruit people who can afford your product. Targeting the wrong users with your research and testing can result in costly redesigns that could have been avoided if more accurate insights had been captured and used early on in the process.

"Any input at all is better than none," you might say, and there is some validity in that. But if I am in desperate tooth pain, I would prefer the input of a dentist to that of a mechanic! The dentist would be much better at helping me overcome my, in this case *literal*, pain points. And only people who *are* your customers, or who are *like* your customers, can help you design products that relieve your customers' pain, providing them with a great user experience.

One of UserZoom's customers, a Fortune 1000 science solutions manufacturing company, recently transitioned to a new responsive website platform. Responsive web design is an approach to web design that makes web pages render well on a variety of devices and window or screen sizes from minimum to maximum display size, across mobile, tablet, laptop, and desktop screen sizes. This change introduced a whole new set of research approaches for its UX team. They are employing UserZoom to conduct a wide range of online usability studies to help refine the website's structure and support international usability testing for the company's 160 countries as well as languages in its four regions—quite a challenge!

This company created a digital advisory panel, using UserZoom's recruiting features to invite users from all over the world to join this panel. Then, based on user profiles, they reach out to different panel members for studies specific to particular tasks, businesses, or countries.

"One of the unique obstacles we face is that it's hard to find our users, and they're very expensive to recruit because they're professionals, they're busy, and they get a ton of email," says a spokesperson for the company. When they want to find participants relevant to specific industries, they can simply narrow the participant panel down to a particular set of criteria and rapidly conduct the study with the right audience. The company spokesperson goes on to say,

> We just did a study with the filtration and purification industry, and we wanted to get feedback on product attributes in the catalog. ... The advisory panel allowed us to quickly find out who's in the filtration industry and send them an email invitation.

> This has allowed us to be lean and mean when it comes to launching the studies. We get feedback much more quickly this way, we create a rapport with these people, they hear from us time and again, and they know we have a dependable system for compensation.

The company plans to expand its digital advisory panel to multiple regions, including Mexico, Brazil, and Asia.

Composing Customer Panels

The traditional challenges with recruiting users for UX research include

- the work or cost (e.g., through an agency) of recruiting the right type of people;

- the hassle of training people on how to participate in UX research, since they've maybe never done it before;

- the logistical challenges with bringing people into physical, in-person studies (or meeting them where they are); and

- the pains involved in making one-off payments.

Recruiting the right people to test your product or service isn't easy. In a recent UserZoom State of UX in the Enterprise survey, we asked UX researchers what phase of the testing process is the most challenging for them. Forty-eight percent of the UX researchers surveyed said that recruiting participants was the most difficult part of the testing process.

Why is this the case? There are a multitude of reasons. Perhaps your product or service is in a narrow niche and therefore not many people in the general population fit your user target. Perhaps your company stakeholders simply don't comprehend the ROI for investing time, effort, and money into recruiting when they heard somewhere that five users will show you 85 percent of the most common usability issues. (There is a lot of misinformation out there.) Perhaps you're a team of one or you're working in agile sprints and think you don't have the bandwidth to find the right people—although the fact is that you really can't afford *not* to get the right people.

Forty-eight percent of the UX research- ers surveyed said that recruiting participants was the most difficult part of the testing process.

This is where composing appropriate user or customer panels comes in. A good user panel is culled from a database of people who have opted in to participate in UX studies. This database has multiple user characteristics that can be searched to find just the right people to participate in your testing.

Sometimes these users are recruited by companies via loyalty programs, so they know that the users testing their products have a vested interest in what the company is producing. These are often ideal customers and therefore good subjects for new products *or* for testing changes in existing products.

Recruiting for customer panels, inviting them to participate in a study, and collecting feedback from them can all be done online now, whereas it used to involve getting people to a physical location or having someone call them in order to vet them—which was much less convenient for them and for the company considering them for a customer panel. Digitally, you can choose people for a research session very quickly and test them quickly, using much less of their time as well as yours. And as I've emphasized previously, the whole recruiting procedure, from invitation to testing to gathering the data to uploading it to the cloud for access, *can now be done automatically using software!*

There are several types of user panels. Here are a few common ones:

1. **General Population (GenPop)**—Also known as "consumer panel," people who represent the "average" person within the population; they have a car, a job, a phone, etc.—whatever qualifies them as an average member of the population you are testing. This kind of panel is good for testing products that almost anyone might use, such as a grocery shopping app, a men's and women's clothing store website, or a general health product.

2. **Specialty or Vertical**—People with very specific profiles: Porsche owners, people with disabilities, homeowners, single mothers, investors—or any other specialized group that is relevant to what you need to test. This kind of panel will be

useful if you have a very clear-cut audience or want to satisfy a very specific need or need to ensure your product conforms to the Americans with Disabilities Act.

3. **Private Community**—A company's own panel of users who have experience with the product and can be good judges of changes to your existing products and of new, complementary products. This kind of panel is very helpful to companies that make frequent updates and test early and often—agile companies—because it makes sense to go back to the same experienced group and ask about potential new or changed features or additional products that align with the existing ones.

4. **Internal**—A company's own employees, who can be used to test out digital products that will be used within the company—such as a new HR website, a business travel planning tool, or a healthcare app.

Companies exist—Vision Critical and Fuel Cycle, for example—that will help you build and maintain private customer panels, making sure that your participants provide you with real value and stay happy doing testing for you on an ongoing basis. They can also help you find fresh participants when you need them—either for a specific kind of testing or just to refresh your testing group, so you're not overwhelming your regular customer panel with tests or testing the same people all the time.

We at UserZoom provide this service for our customers, too, because we understand just how important it is to have the right kind of participants available for customer panels. Our customers can go online on our website and say what they want to test and what kind of people they need to test and how many of those people are required.

We quickly form the customer panel for them from the database, and then they can launch their test for that panel and get the results of the test very quickly. So a customer can wake up with an idea they want to test out, put out the test that very day, and get results *within a few hours to a day.* It's like magic! This is what automated UX research has made possible. This is why so many more companies are doing this kind of research on a regular, frequent basis now. All of our customers use panels, and many of them do UX testing weekly.

It is also important in our global digital culture that you test your products internationally. You want your products to be as effective in Italy or Japan as they are in the United States. Companies that specialize in building customer panels can make sure that you have high-quality test participants from around the world.

In order to get people to participate in your panels, you often need to reward them—with cash or PayPal cards or Amazon gift cards or something along those lines. However, because rewards are offered, you must also have the means to qualify people before adding them to your testing database to ensure that they are not just participating in order to get the reward! There are multiple ways to check the identities of participants, such as via PayPal and/or LinkedIn, where only one account is allowed, to be sure that the participant is legitimate. A company such as Imperium can help you establish tight security for your panels, so your participants can be confident that their identity and their responses are kept confidential.

Finally, there are also best practices for ensuring that people are going through the study in

So a customer can wake up with an idea they want to test out, put out the test that very day, and get results *within a few hours to a day.*

a "normal" way, not rushing through at abnormally fast speeds or choosing answers at random. We call this "sample quality control." For example, UserZoom's software allows researchers to block speeders (automatically exclude participants who do not spend enough time taking a navigation task) and cheaters (automatically exclude participants who do not make enough clicks while taking a navigation task), eliminating their responses from the results collected.

Research Goals and Sample Sizes

Another consideration is how many people you want on a panel, and that depends on the kind of information you're seeking. In the previous chapter, I talked about the difference between quantitative and qualitative data, and which of those you're seeking determines how many users you need to involve in your research.

Let's say you're trying to discern user attitudes toward a certain software feature. Do they like this feature or not? Do they think this feature is really going to help them or not? That's going to be an opinion. For that, you're going to want to run a survey to determine how valuable the feature is for them, say on a scale from one to five, five being most valuable and one being not valuable at all. For this kind of survey, it doesn't make sense to run it with just ten people. There's a concept called margin of error, and you want to make sure that this margin is as low as possible. So typically, for a survey you should have a hundred people or two hundred people or even more. With this size of customer panel, you'll feel more confident about the results, because if a hundred people responded and eighty people are saying they don't like it, you know there's a problem.

But this quantitative approach doesn't make sense—and is unnecessary—for a more in-depth task-based study to uncover behavior and qualitative information, to learn *why* people do what they do. For that, you need to have an interaction, a dialogue, and be able to ask questions or actually observe how users are doing things or both. It's impractical to do this with a hundred or two hundred people. You really only need between five and ten (typically five per user type is enough) for this kind of exploration. You're going to ask this group to go into your website or your app and try to find a particular kind of information or try to send a message or try to do a series of tasks. And then you're going to observe what they do and how they do it and ask them questions. "Why did you go here? Why did you click that? How did you feel about working with this part of the product?"

If you sent a survey, you would just get one to five answers—and perhaps you could ask an open-ended question—but it's not the same as observing a user in action and having a one-on-one conversation with that user in the moment. You just can't get that with a survey. You're not trying to quantify things in this kind of research. You're trying to get a feel for how things work for people and where and, very importantly, why they don't work for them.

Now, if you talk to ten people, and eight of them have an issue working with a feature, you could then launch a survey to two hundred people and have them try the feature on their own without anybody looking at them and then rate their experience. And that's where you can quantify the extent of a feature's problem. Alternatively, you could actually try to address the problem identified by the eight people first, then retest before sending it off to two hundred. Either one is fine.

How big does your testing sample need to be? That question can be compared to someone showing you the following illustration and asking you what kind of tool they should use:

What tool do I need?

Of course, your first question would be, What are you trying to accomplish? And the same question needs to be asked about what you're trying to accomplish with your testing. Depending on your intended outcomes, here are UserZoom's recommendations about sample size. In dark gray is the most common set of numbers we see across hundreds and hundreds of studies:

WHAT SAMPLE SIZE DO I NEED?

Identifying Usability Issues		Estimating Parameters KPI		Comparing Options		
Problem/ Insight Occurrence	Sample Size Needed	Margin of Error (+/-)	Sample Size Needed 90% Confidence	Difference to Detect 90% Confidence	Sample Size within Subjects	Sample Size between Subjects
40%	4	24%	10	50%	17	22
30%	5	15%	28	30%	29	64
20%	9	10%	65	12%	93	426
10%	18	8%	103	10%	115	614
5%	37	5%	268	5%	246	2,468
		3%	749	3%	421	6,866
		2%	1,689	1%	1,297	61,822

Tips for Composing Customer Panels

Yes, recruiting can be tricky, but there are ways to make it easier and get it right. Here are five tips for doing that:

1. **Overrecruit**—If you recruit ten test subjects, know that at least one out of the ten will bow out—probably at the last minute. Always have a few backups.

2. **Account for recruiting time in your planning**—Don't underestimate the amount of time it will take to recruit your subjects—UX teams do it all the time. Start by asking questions: Are the target subjects rare? Do we have some on file already? Do you need live users from your site? Historically, has it taken a lot of effort to find subjects? Do we need to recruit from an entirely new segment of users? Should we handle finding subjects in house, or should we use a panel vendor?

3. **Determine if your subjects need technical knowledge**— Don't assume that your recruits have some kind of technical knowledge or expertise—screen for it (and don't make assumptions about which subjects don't have it either). If recruits need a particular piece of software, hardware, or other equipment, make sure they have it.

4. **Take compensation into account**—Show respect for people's time. The longer the study, the more in depth it is, and the more technical the task required, the higher the compensation it's likely to require. If you're not getting the number of completes you need in the expected time you've allotted, take a fresh look at what you're asking subjects to do and what you're offering in return. Also be aware that not everyone is motivated by money. Is there another way to

make people interested in participating? Maybe a potential recruit doesn't want the gift card but would be delighted if it were donated to a charity of her choice in her name.

5. **Always use a screener**—Even if you're doing live intercepts from a page on your website that is literally a fan club, use a screener to vet the subjects you get. This will help safeguard your data and also ensure that all the work you or the panel provider has done isn't wasted when you have to go back and vet participants and find that you have to rerecruit.

Let's go into more detail about screening, because it's important. Here are ten tips for effective screening:

1. **Keep the screener short and precise!** Do not ask more than five questions, or participants will tend to get disengaged and drop out. Asking too many questions, particularly when targeting niche profiles, may lead to "panelist fatigue," an industry term used to describe the frustration experienced by participants.

2. **Provide incentive.** If the screening is expected to be complex or longer than expected, offer an incentive to participants who complete a short screening but do not qualify for the longer one. It is very frustrating for panelists to get screened out at the last moment after spending five minutes going through the questions. A small incentive can build trust among your panelists and encourage them to not give up.

3. **Stay away from the single-choice questions.** Use multiple-answer instead of single-answer questions. With single-answer questions, participants have a 50 percent chance of qualifying, which decreases the credibility of the screening. This also helps screen out participants who will lie just to qualify for the project.

DON'T ASK	ASK
Do you work in market research? [One Answer] • Yes • No	Which of these fields do you work in? [Multiple Answers] • Finance • Market Research • Technology • Healthcare • Food & Beverage • Other • I am a student • I am retired/I am a veteran • I am unemployed

4. **Do not ask leading questions.** Leading questions could influence an individual to provide a particular response. Answers chosen from a list you provide are more reliable.

DON'T ASK	ASK
On a scale of 1–5, how much do you like using Netflix?	On a scale of 1–5, how do you feel about using Netflix?
Are you considering getting a mortgage in the next 12 months • Yes • No	Which of the following life events are you considering in the next 12 months? • Buying a car • Getting a mortgage • Having a baby • Getting a pet • Continuing my education • Traveling • Retiring • Other

5. **Use clear and concise language.** Avoid sentences that could confuse participants. Avoid jargon, acronyms, or abbreviations (unless you define them, and the target participants are likely to know them). Once you've sent out an online survey, you will not have an opportunity to clarify it. Therefore, it is imperative that participants can understand the language on their own.

6. **Be specific when defining frequencies.** Asking questions with answer choices such as often, rarely, sometimes, etc. is confusing and subjective. Some participants may define often as once a week, while others may define it as every day. Specificity gives you more useful data.

DON'T ASK	ASK
How frequently do you use MsOffice? • Rarely • Often • Sometimes	How frequently do you use MsOffice? • Daily • Weekly • A few times in a month • Rarely • Never

7. **Use the "other" option.** Provide the option for participants to select "other," "I don't know," or "none of the above" as answer options when a list is not all encompassing. This will yield better data by preventing participants from selecting inaccurate answers just so they can proceed to the next question.

8. **Provide clear answer choices.** Avoid answers that overlap or cause confusion. A common example is overlapping age or income-bracket answer choices.

DON'T ASK	ASK
What is your age? • Under 18 • 18–24 • 24–34 • 34–44 • 44–54 • 54–64 • Over 64 In this example, participants aged 24/34/44/54/64 will not know whether to select the former or the latter answer choice.	What is your age? • Under 18 • 18–24 • 25–34 • 35–44 • 45–54 • 55–64 • 65 or over

9. **Limit the number of open-ended questions.** Asking too many open-ended questions leads to panelist fatigue and dropouts. Participants tend to type gibberish when they are forced to answer too many, or too repetitive, open-ended questions. Many open-ended questions also require the researcher to read through hundreds of responses, manually determining who qualifies.

10. **Edit, test, and revise.** Edit and revise your screener at least twice before using it widely. Test your screener yourself by going through it and submitting real answers. Then send it to colleagues and ask them to do the same. This process will help you target the data you need, understand what it feels like to answer the questions, and eliminate extraneous questions.

There are many moving parts to consider when putting together a UX study to ensure that it's successful. Writing a screener is one of the first vital steps. It takes practice to make clear, efficient screeners, but it's necessary so you can be sure your target users are represented in your studies.

─────────────── **KEY TAKEAWAYS** ───────────────

▶ Real feedback from real people is essential to the success of UX research. The quality of your results is dependent on the quality of the people you test. Quality means that these people fit your target product audience profile as closely as possible.

▶ A good user panel is culled from a database of people who have opted in to participate in UX studies. This database has multiple user characteristics that can be searched to find just the right people to participate in your testing.

▶ The whole recruiting procedure, from invitations to testing to gathering the data to uploading it to the cloud for access, *can now be done automatically using software*, using one of the companies that provides these services.

▶ The sample size and research method will vary greatly depending, ultimately, on the kind of information you're seeking or the research goals.

▶ Recruiting the right people to test your product or service isn't always easy, but there are ways to make it easier and more effective, and again, there are companies that provide participant recruiting and screening services for composing customer panels.

CHAPTER 7

Measuring the Benefits and ROI of Delivering Exceptional Digital Experiences

The web is the ultimate customer-empowering environment. He or she who clicks the mouse gets to decide everything. It is so easy to go elsewhere; all the competitors in the world are but a mouse click away.
—JAKOB NIELSEN, NIELSON NORMAN GROUP

I n a digital experience company, great UX design is your best "salesperson." Your customers or potential customers are going to check out your app or your website, and if they like it, if they have a good experience, they'll move forward with your company. If they don't, they'll leave. It's as simple as that in the digital age. So if you don't have a great product UX, you're not going to get the customers you should be getting, or you're going to lose the customers you have over time.

I talked earlier about the financial benefits of paying close attention to UX design research and producing a great customer experience—about how being a great digital experience company leads to success. To quote a *Forbes* article, "Forrester Research shows that, on average, every dollar invested in UX brings 100 dollars in return. That's an ROI of a whopping 9,900 percent."[28]

But how do you determine whether or not your UX design is leading to financial success and whether it is producing a customer experience that will enable your success over the long term? In order to determine this, you need to do more than test usability; you need to take your process to the next level and implement a solid, reliable UX success measurement program.

Financial and experiential success with a UX is analogous to the difference between qualitative and quantitative testing that we delineated in the previous chapter: one has to do with experience and the other with numbers. Both are essential to your company's success as a digital experience company. If you want to identify and understand what's happening for your company in both of these areas, you need to think about it not just from a UX testing perspective but from a UX success measurement perspective. You need to define the appropriate key performance indicators (KPIs) and determine how your UX design is actually impacting those KPIs.

You need to do more than test usability; you need to take your process to the next level and implement a solid, reliable UX success measurement program.

A Nielson Norman Group article on calculating UX design ROI breaks it down to a four-step

---

28   Andrew Kucheriavy, "Good UX Is Good Business: How to Reap Its Benefits," *Forbes*, November 19, 2015, https://www.forbes.com/sites/forbestechcouncil/2015/11/19/good-ux-is-good-business-how-to-reap-its-benefits/?sh=e3713c24e51d

process:[29]

1. Collect a UX metric in a benchmarking study.

2. Choose a KPI.

3. Convert the UX metric into the KPI.

4. Report the calculation responsibly.

In the following section, I'll lay out the kind of UX metrics you should measure.

Measuring UX Design Metrics

A great UX design should provide many benefits, but you need to measure those benefits in order to ensure that your UX is delivering what it ought to deliver. These benefits/metrics are as follows:

- Lower cost of customer acquisition

- Lower cost of support

- Improved internal productivity (such as employee)

- Increased customer retention

- De-risking of product development process (or reducing product failure before it goes live)

- Increased market share

These are the areas where great digital experience companies consistently do well. In order to become that kind of company, you need to know if your UX design is enabling you to do well in all of them.

---

29   Kate Moran, "Calculating ROI for Design Projects in 4 Steps," February 23, 2020, Norman Nielson Group, https://www.nngroup.com/articles/calculating-roi-design-projects/.

LOWER COST OF CUSTOMER ACQUISITION

As I've said, your product experience should be your best salesperson. If that experience is good for potential users, your product will sell itself. This is commonly called product-led growth (PLG). Once you get these potential customers to try your app or website through traditional sales methods such as direct sales, the UX then becomes the sales pitch; it convinces your customers to either keep coming back or drop away and find another company with a better user experience to satisfy their needs. You shift marketing dollars from traditional sales/marketing to UX design and testing in order to accomplish this, to make sure the potential customer is being sold to by the product itself.

A good UX also solidifies customers' interactions with traditional salespeople; it motivates them to go back to the salesperson because of their good experience with the product. Marketing is expensive. You can shoot a thousand bullets to hit one target. But when you bring people to your website or app, if they don't have a great product experience there, it's all for nothing—it's one and done. They move on. So a great UX will most certainly help make your marketing campaign more efficient.

Google is a great example of how effective a great UX can be. We all know that the company has grown like crazy and become a worldwide success. But back in the day, *they didn't even do traditional marketing*. Their success was based on how well they did what the user needed them to do. It was an amazing experience compared to what had come before. You could just find stuff—almost anything, it seemed! And the way they designed their incredibly minimalistic home page and the results page was user friendly; everything was well put together to solve the user's problem of needing solid information quickly. So people kept coming back and coming back—to the point where "googling" became a verb that people substituted for searching online, because it was the *best* way to search online. A great UX, including superior search results, sold the product all on its own.

LOWER COST OF SUPPORT

Successful digital experience companies understand that their users don't want to pick up the phone or write an email to support; they want to be able to help themselves. This is a good thing for these companies, because it lowers their cost of support. But this will only happen if the app or website is so easy to use that it prevents users from *having to* get in touch with support. There's a level of expectation among today's users that they'll only have to get in touch with support if they have to do something complicated. Otherwise, they want to be able to help themselves—and the best digital experience companies understand that.

Amazon is great at this. They've designed their website to provide customers with ways they can help themselves, whether that's getting more information on a product, changing or canceling an order, changing a home address or other profile information, and so on. This is ultimately what lowers their support costs. Amazon proactively looks for ways to provide their users with the means to accomplish what they need to accomplish—getting more information on a product, changing or canceling an order, changing a home address or other profile information, and so on. They've designed the site to allow users to do their thing—which helps turn new users into customers and retains existing customers.

Here is an old example but one I think is still relevant: McAfee redesigned its ProtectionPilot software (from the enterprise side of the business, which is no longer part of McAfee) in 2004 to improve its usability. And when they launched it, their tech support calls decreased by 90 percent. They had twenty thousand downloads over a ten-week period, and there were only 170 support calls.[30]

Another example of how to engender high support costs was my own experience with the clothing retailer, which I mentioned in chapter 1. Due to a poor UX, which lacked important information about product availability, I ended up having to talk to their phone support several times. A more effective search experience would have allowed me to complete my task, to find out whether or not the clothing I was interested in was in stock, right on the spot.

Website or app visitors are used to convenience and usability now. They expect it and demand it! If a website or app doesn't allow them to complete what they came to do in both an effective and efficient way, they're going to reach out to customer support—and customer support centers are expensive. By being proactive with UX design, companies avoid having streams of people vying for customer support's attention, taking up support's expensive time. This is not to say that you don't need to have a great customer support team. That's still very important, because, when it *is* used, it's an important part of the customer experience. But great UX design is the best ally for your customer support team, because it reduces their workload—while reducing your support costs—and enables the team to focus on the kind of problems that can *only* be handled by support, not ones that users could handle themselves if the product made it easy for them to do that.

An article by UI designer Chris Zink sums it up simply: "A well-designed app just *works*. If an application is poorly designed, there will be an increased need for training, documentation, and support later, which translates into higher costs. An app that is intuitive and easy to use puts less stress on both employees and the bottom line. "[31]

---

30 "The Business Value of User Experience," Infragistics, January 2014, https://www. infragistics.com/media/335732/the_business_value_of_user_experience-3.pdf.

31 Chris Zink and Cority Enviance, "5 Benefits of Great UI/UX Design," October 3, 2017, https://www.enviance.com/blog/benefits-of-great-enterprise-ui/ux-design.

INCREASED PRODUCTIVITY

Great digital experience companies see their employees as "customers" too. They make a serious investment in UX design and testing for the internal apps they build or adopt that their employees need to use frequently. They do this because they understand the value of their employees' time as well as the value of their customers' time. Having tools that make it easy to accomplish HR and payroll and health insurance tasks frees up time that enables employees to be more productive. This is especially true of larger companies, where wasted employee time multiplies rapidly across the company on a daily basis. If a hundred salespeople are saving forty hours per year on such tasks, the company has gained a hundred weeks of productivity—and that's a great ROI for investing in apps that provide a good UX!

An app that is intuitive and easy to use puts less stress on both employees and the bottom line.

SaaS companies such as Workday, Namely, and Expensify offer HR- and administration-related products that can help you do this. These cloud-based digital experience companies are revolutionizing the HR market with applications that let employees accomplish employment-related tasks themselves quickly and easily, anytime, anywhere—even from their smartphones. Sales is an important area where this is effective. By giving salespeople products that make tasks such as arranging travel and reporting expenses easier, you free up more of their time for selling. And the same is true for employees in all areas of your company. Whatever their responsibilities for the company, they can accomplish more when they have apps that allow them to complete employment-related tasks more efficiently. You can benchmark how much time employees put into repetitive tasks, and after introducing easy-to-use digital products to accomplish those tasks, you can measure again and quantify the cost versus amount of time saved—the ROI.

INCREASED CUSTOMER RETENTION AND EXPANSION

Great UX keeps customers coming back! And as I said earlier, with more and more digital companies moving to the SaaS model, customer retention becomes increasingly important. With the SaaS model, if customers are unhappy with the UX, they can unsubscribe and go elsewhere instantly—and they're not shy about doing it! It's not like they've brought a product home or are using it at work and will necessarily hang on to it for years, as they did in the past. They're using the product online, week to week, month to month, and they want to be able to accomplish what they need to accomplish easily and intuitively—and they will ditch the product the moment it becomes more hassle to use than it's worth to them and find a better online product.

This is great for the customer, but it can be disastrous for SaaS companies, because they've made a huge investment to develop the product and acquire customers and must continue to invest to maintain and update the product. But when the subscription period is annual, they only get one-twelfth of their annual revenue per month, so they stand to lose a great deal of revenue through early churn or cancellation of the subscription at the end of the term, because customers aren't satisfied with the UX.

Business growth expert Lincoln Murphy sums up the downside and upside of the SaaS model this way:

> So the reality around Customer Churn is that for every customer you lose through attrition, cancellations, or non-

renewals—you have to acquire one new customer just to break even …

Consequently, if you want to grow, you need to acquire TWO new customers just to grow by ONE net new customer …

On the flip side, retaining customers for a longer period of time increases the profitability of that customer, but not just by keeping them paying the same thing for the entire lifetime.

No, customers who stay longer are more likely to not just stay a customer, but to pay you more—above the sales price they originally signed-on at—as they continue to use more and more of your SaaS application—what's called Expansion Revenue.[32]

Since a customer's perception of value from a SaaS company is directly linked to how self-serviceable the product is, a great product UX has a significant impact on whether or not a SaaS customer will stay around. To find out if a refined UX achieves this, you can set a retention ratio benchmark and then introduce the new UX and measure the change in customer retention, in churn, over time to see if you're keeping more customers for longer periods of time.

A great UX will also encourage people who continue using your product to recommend that product to their colleagues. There are often "tryouts" of new products within parts of a customer organization, and if those tryouts are successful, the word spreads quickly! If eight out of a hundred people use and like the product, their manager is going to realize that the product will be used and will help people

---

32 Lincoln Murphy, "SaaS Customer Retention Is the Key to Long-term Profitability," Customer-Centric Growth by Lincoln Murphy, https://sixteenventures.com/customer-retention-profitability.

do better work, motivating that manager to recommend adoption throughout that part of the organization—and, if appropriate, organization-wide.

DE-RISKING THE PRODUCT DEVELOPMENT PROCESS

In the same Cority Enviance article I quoted above, Chris Zink says the following:

> An estimated 50% of engineering time is spent redoing work to fix mistakes that could have been avoided, like incorrect assumptions about how users will behave, confusing navigation that causes users to get stuck or lost, a new feature that nobody wants to use, or a design choice that isn't accessible. Making sure the design is done right—and done well—the first time around will prevent future headaches.[33]

"Making sure the design is done right" is achieved through solid UX research throughout the development process. Earlier in the book, I outlined the agile development process, which is used by successful digital experience companies. The agile approach means developing products iteratively, and part of what is constantly reiterated is UX testing. It requires allocating time to do continuous testing, usually on a weekly basis. In the past, you would develop a product for a long time and then maybe test it once, in detail, and go live. This meant that if you made mistakes, you'd only discover them months into the development process, and then you'd have to go back and fix them—a much more difficult and expensive job, at that point.

With the agile approach, you uncover UX mistakes and problems during every step of the process. You won't be 100 percent certain about all UX aspects of a product when you release it, even with this

---

33   Chris Zink and Cority Enviance, "5 Benefits of Great UI/UX Design."

approach, but your level of certainty will be *much* higher, because you've been testing it out all along, correcting mistakes and solving problems. And you'll have gathered feedback on the product that will make you much more confident that it will succeed with users.

I have been part of many digital product development processes where we had to go back and change features and functions a long way into the process, and I can tell you that it is extremely expensive and time consuming. Today, great digital experience companies don't risk that happening. They get the user feedback they need by embedding UX research in the development process. To my mind, *not* doing this is almost like purposely spending more on building the product than you need to for a product.

With the agile approach, you uncover UX mistakes and problems during every step of the process.

INCREASED MARKET SHARE

Obviously, this is the ultimate goal of creating a product with a great UX design: it will appeal to such a broad group of users that your share of the market in your industry will increase. And this success will be measured by the traditional means of measuring market share. I talked above about how a great UX is your best salesperson, and that will be borne out if your product is used widely and reviewed well and shared via enthusiastic word-of-mouth recommendations. This is the ultimate payoff for the time and money you've invested in developing a great UX design. A product with this kind of UX is sometimes referred to as a "killer app." Paying close attention to UX research will help you "slay" your competition!

INCREASED INNOVATION

Last but certainly not least, I want to highlight the value of conducting UX research for innovation purposes. As Steve Jobs famously said at an Apple developer conference, "You've got to start with the customer experience and work backwards to the technology."

We all know how important it is to continuously innovate and adapt to change. As the world continues to move faster and technology evolves more quickly, consultancies and corporations are increasingly concentrating on their innovation strategies.

Conducting user research is an extremely important aspect of innovation—both in generating ideas for new and innovative products and in guiding the development of products from their inception to their release. User experience research can be an instrumental tool in the alignment of customer wants and needs with the future goals of a strategic vision.

It's really all about staying ahead of the game, gathering insights on market trends and future customer preferences. Here's an example from WillowTree, which builds digital products:

Finding a Point of Differentiation for Entering the Market

by Matthew Morrison, Senior Product Researcher

- **The Challenge:** "A client asked us to come up with an app idea that would appeal to first-time Millennial mothers. Because we knew that tracker apps like BabyCenter were already popular, we wanted to find a way that our client could set themselves apart and gain traction in the market."

- **The Research:** "When we began interviewing first-time mothers from different backgrounds, we found that mothers are overwhelmed by the amount of advice on how to raise children. To cope, many moms eschew large anonymous baby forums and instead opt for more intimate online forums where they know the other moms. For example, many moms created private Facebook groups for moms in their region to share experiences. These moms trusted the advice of other moms because they could see when they had connections to other moms through mutual friends. In other words, mothers trusted and listened to the advice given by other moms who were in their extended social networks."

- **The Outcome:** "We realized that our client could make space for themselves in the market by building an app that would use the trust inherent in social networks to deliver content to moms by allowing them to view each other's mutual friends, exchange advice, and possibly meet up."[34]

Benchmarking the User Experience

UX design teams have long struggled to come up with a single user experience benchmarking score to share with the development team and other stakeholders. They have needed something that would allow

---

34   Claire Maiers, PhD, "Five Real-World Examples of the Value of User Research," WillowTree, March 25, 2020, https://willowtreeapps.com/ideas/five-real-world-examples-of-the-value-of-user-research.

them to measure user experience consistently and quantitatively and produce something that could be easily understood at a glance.

Unfortunately, this is not as simple a task as one might assume.

When searching for the way to quantify user experiences, the kinds of questions that come up include the following:

- What metrics should be included?

- How can we create a repeatable, apples-to-apples benchmarking score?

- How can we make this score simple and easy to understand for even the least UX-savvy executive?

Achieving this can be challenging, but we have developed one excellent tool at my company, UserZoom, and we also use others that are easily available to aggregate and analyze user responses to their experience and produce results that are easy to understand.

THE QXSCORE

At UserZoom, we did *a lot* of UX benchmarking, so we had a lot of time to ponder these questions. Eventually, we came up with the concept of an overall quality of experience score, which we call the QXscore. Its purpose is to create a single benchmarking score for any digital product. This is an experience score that combines various measurements, collecting both behavioral data (such as task success) and attitudinal data (such as ease of use, trust, and response to the appearance of the product). Once we enter data into our UX scorecard calculator, we can generate a QXscorecard that looks like this:

Quality of Experience Score Rance (UZIndex):	Very Poor >45	Poor 45-60	Average 61-75	Good 76-90	Great 91-100
Task 1: First Impressions					100%
Task 2: Find + Print Account Info	39%				
Task 3: View Recent Trx				83%	
Task 4: Change Address			66%		
Task 5: Find Wholesaler Info					95%
Usability (ease of use)			67%		
Trust					94%
Appearance		59%			
Loyalty		56%			

Behavior: What they did (Task Success)

Attitudes: What they feel, say

qxScore: 72

* **Task Success:** Percentage of users that completed the task successfully.
* **Attitudes:** The four attitudes are based on eight questions, two per category and represents "top 2" box percentage rating.
* Task success was coded manually based on screen recordings. N=18 for task 1, n=6 for the rest of the task.

The number in the circle in this example, seventy-two, is the user experience score for this particular product. Going deeper, you can see the individual scores for experience areas such as trust and appearance. In this example, trust is strong, but appearance needs some work.

The QXscore is a simple, clear, and persuasive tool for communicating user research results to everyone involved in product development. In this case, presenting a clear score of seventy-two out of one hundred makes it easy for even the least UX-savvy stakeholders to grasp the current state of users' experience of the product.

This is important, because getting executive buy-in for UX research spending can be difficult when they don't clearly understand the results that are being achieved by it. Being able to quickly and easily get your point across to stakeholders—for example, showing them that the previous QXscore was sixty-three and now it's up to seventy-two—will help get buy-in for continued benchmarking. Equally important, it helps the development team and the company at large understand where to focus and what to prioritize in the development process.

SUS: SYSTEM USABILITY SCALE

According to the Nielsen Norman Group,

> The most well-known questionnaire used in UX research is the System Usability Scale (SUS). The SUS has been around since the command-line interface days of the 1980s, and has been repeatedly demonstrated experimentally to be valid and reliable. It was invented by John Brooke at Digital Equipment Corporation. The SUS is a post-test instrument, given to a participant after an entire usability testing session is over (or, when testing multiple sites, like in competitive evaluations, after the participant has worked on all the tasks related to a site).[35]

---

35   Page Laubheimer, "Beyond the NPS: Measuring Perceived Usability with the SUS, NASA-TLX, and the Single Ease Question after Tasks and Usability Tests," Nielson Norman Group, February 11, 2019, https://www.nngroup.com/articles/measuring-perceived-usability/.

With the SUS, for every website usability test carried out, users complete a short questionnaire and a score is derived from that. It's on a Likert scale, which helps to ascribe a quantitative value to qualitative opinions. The questions are easily responded to by selecting an option from "strongly agree" to "strongly disagree."

1. The website has a user-friendly interface.

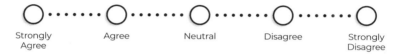

Strongly Agree   Agree   Neutral   Disagree   Strongly Disagree

2. The website is easy to navigate.

Strongly Agree   Agree   Neutral   Disagree   Strongly Disagree

The benefits of this measurement are that it's very easy to administer, can be used on a small sample size, and can clearly indicate whether a feature has improved or not. However, bear in mind that the scoring system is complex, and it won't tell you what's wrong with your site; it merely classifies its ease of use.

You can learn more about the SUS at https://www.usability.gov/how-to-and-tools/methods/system-usability-scale.html.

SUPR-Q: STANDARDIZED USER EXPERIENCE PERCENTILE RANK QUESTIONNAIRE

This is an eight-item questionnaire for measuring the quality of the website user experience. According to MeasuringU, which licenses the SUPR-Q, the questionnaire helps you learn about the following areas:

- **Usability:** If users can't accomplish what they want to do, find the product they're looking for, or complete their purchase, it's as if the information or product doesn't exist. A usable experience means a profitable experience.

- **Credibility (Trust, Value, and Comfort):** Does the website sell products and collect credit card information? Are you gathering email addresses to build a subscriber base? If users don't trust your website, which for many companies is synonymous with their company and brand, they won't give up their information and website growth is impeded.

- **Loyalty:** Are users talking about your website favorably or are they telling their friends to avoid it like the plague? Will they return to the website and purchase more, or at least see what you have to say? The two questions asked under Loyalty touch on repeat usage from existing customers and net-new usage from new customers.

- **Appearance:** Is your website looking like it's circa 1998, or is the appearance hindering the experience? Users form impressions of your website based on the appearance in just a few seconds.[36]

You can learn more about SUPR-Q at www.suprq.com.

At UserZoom customer Kimberly-Clark, Yuan Zhou, global UX design lead, made it her mission to tie the impact of UX directly to the company's bottom line. A major redesign was planned for one of the company's digital properties geared to business buyers, so she wanted to ensure that the team had a way not only to measure improvements but also to learn how to further optimize design.

---

36   "Super-Q Full License," MeasuringU, https://measuringu.com/product/suprq/.

Good UX design is meant to be invisible, so Yuan was struggling with how to measure the impact of major design changes over time and communicate the results effectively to key stakeholders across her organization.

Most of the metrics her team was tracking, using website analytics and NPS surveys, weren't meaningful measures of UX. NPS was an attitudinal measure of loyalty and didn't incorporate how users actually behaved. And while site analytics accounted for how users behaved, many factors outside of the experience could impact the analytics. To get a holistic measure specific to the impact of UX on key business metrics, she needed a score that incorporated both what users were doing and how they felt about the company's site, products, or features. Most commonly used ways to measure UX rely only on responses—what users say and feel—or only on behaviors—what users do.

Yuan was looking for a measurement framework that allowed her to cascade organizational goals down to product goals and ultimately to translate those into meaningful measures of UX. That way there would be alignment across stakeholders on how UX can impact the overall business and how that would be operationalized.

So, she turned to UserZoom's QXscore, described above, as a meaningful, easily understood standard for measuring user experience that aligns to strategic business KPIs and identifies tactical areas to improve UX health. It quantified users' attitudes and behaviors into a single score that could be used to track progress over time, relative to competitors, or across multiple lines of business, digital properties, and products. This would make it easy for business leaders to evaluate UX performance while providing digital experience stakeholders with insights into how to improve the UX.

Yuan's team measured progress over time with the QXscore—before and after the redesign. This allowed them to take into account specific user behaviors that impacted sales and support costs, along with attitudinal measures such as ease of use. The end result was a single metric that the team shared with stakeholders to track and prove how the changes in UX from the redesign impacted business outcomes.

Now, says Yuan, "We can easily track and improve how UX research can impact business outcomes."

Another UserZoom customer, Adobe, used the QXscore to measure behavioral and attitudinal data to confidently drive further improvements to its Experience Cloud product and create data-driven customer value.

Pert Eilers, senior program manager, product operations, for Adobe's Experience Cloud, explains that this was Adobe's first foray into systematic user behavior measuring of this kind, and it was going to be used for all the products for which the company did UX benchmarking. Previously, stakeholders had relied on NPS scores to evaluate the UX, but as Eilers puts it,

> An NPS score is valuable for measuring loyalty and people's attitudes, but it doesn't really tell you what people are actually doing in your product. ... People really like Adobe products ... they would be failing at the task, but would still give us these super high scores. ... So, that was really when I started looking for some ways to bring in the behavioral part of it.

Once they started gathering this behavioral data, they could leverage it to figure out where they needed to apply their design energy to make improvements. Ultimately, the stakeholders were delighted to have the ability to measure UX this way, and they were able to see clear improvement between the first and second iterations of Experience Cloud.

Now, says Eilers, "We know what's working; we know what's not working as well; and we can focus our energies in the right places."

One other opportunity with benchmarks is to find their relationship to common business metrics that companies care about, like conversion rate, NPS, or revenue. Taking it a step further, if a causal connection can be made between the benchmark and the business metrics, you have a road map of how to improve the business by improving the UX.

KEY TAKEAWAYS

► In a digital experience company, great UX design is your best "salesperson."

► To determine whether or not your UX design is leading to financial success, you need to implement a solid, reliable UX success measurement program.

► Calculating UX design ROI breaks it down to a four-step process:

▷ Collect a UX metric in a benchmarking study

▷ Choose a KPI

▷ Convert the UX metric into the KPI

▷ Report the calculation responsibly

► The UX design benefits/metrics you need to quantify are these:

▷ Lower cost of customer acquisition

▷ Lower cost of support

▷ Improved productivity

▷ Increased customer retention

▷ De-risking of product development process

▷ Increased market share

▶ An overall quality of experience score, such as the QXscore, SUS, SUPR-Q, and others we employ at UserZoom, enables you to help the least UX-savvy stakeholders grasp the current state of users' experience of the product and its impact on the product's success.

CHAPTER 8

The Future for Digital Experience Companies: Experience Insights Management

*Coming together is a beginning. Keeping together
is progress. Working together is success.*
—HENRY FORD

*In today's complex and fast-moving world, what we need
even more than foresight or hindsight is insight.*
—ANONYMOUS

The previous chapters of the book were focused mostly on what businesses should do to become successful digital experience (DX) companies, and why offering great digital product experiences is critical to staying relevant and competitive in the marketplace. This included a clear demonstration of the high return on investment (ROI) and the business value and benefits from delivering both great user experience (UX) and great customer experience (CX).

We also addressed product design and research methodologies, as well as the metrics that will help you understand the quality of the digital experience. To deliver great design is actually very difficult. A successful DX company needs to be data driven and to invest in solid UX research. UX designers and engineers are not magicians; they need research on which to base their design and functionality decisions, and they need the support of the whole organization. "It takes a village …" We established that defining, measuring, and benchmarking KPIs are essential to determining how your overall digital product experience is affecting your business and how well you stack up versus your competition.

Now, in this last chapter, we're going to look ahead. I'm going to tell you what I anticipate companies on their way to becoming digital experience companies, as well as some that are already advanced in their journeys, will need to work on to succeed going forward. I'm going to lay out a particular challenge they will encounter and how they can overcome it over the next few years.

Making Data Manageable across the Entire Business

The history of customer relationship management (CRM) spans many decades and culminates in what almost all businesses, large or small, rely on today—a set of processes and systems designed to seamlessly automate and manage customer relationships across departments and business units. Prior to the move to CRM software and then cloud-based technologies, businesses had no centralized way in which to do this. Data such as customer contact details and purchase records lived separate lives in accounts departments, filing cabinets, and salespeople's heads, creating unnecessary inefficiencies and a poor customer experience.

Today's businesses are now facing the same challenge with managing their digital experience. Critical customer journeys (such as signing up for a free trial, returning an item, or making a purchase on a mobile app) increasingly touch multiple areas of the business within a single digital session—from marketing to product to support and beyond. And the multitude of data gathered from this is as overwhelming as it is valuable. Customer service call centers, marketing surveys, usability research, product analytics … user and customer data is being generated minute upon minute, creating nuggets of insight swamped by a deluge of noise. We spoke about data overload at the beginning of the book. The challenge is bringing it all together, winnowing it, organizing it, classifying it, sharing it, and making it searchable—so it can be accessed and actioned by anybody who needs it, at the right time. And often, during website or app development, a company has only days or even hours to analyze this mass of data and apply it to design decisions! (See the description of agile development in chapter 3 to review why this is true.)

To add to the challenge, this data is flowing into separate silos across the business, where it remains inaccessible to the various players that must collaborate to improve these customer journeys. For example, product team members tend to focus on UX (prelive, during design stages) while marketing, customer success, and customer support tend to focus on CX (after the product is live and the users are customers). Too often, the research results found by one area of the company are never shared with other areas of the company—I've been told by customers that they've discovered two parts of their company were essentially running the same kind of research on the same application! But ultimately everyone is working toward the same goal: a great overall end-to-end experience for whomever is using the software.

The net result? A distorted and fragmented view of the overall digital experience that makes it impossible to measure and improve within individual departments, let alone on a strategic level. By eliminating those silos and increasing collaboration and data sharing, teams can gain better visibility on the overall quality of the digital experience at different stages of the product life cycle, and leadership can get a top-down view of how their business's digital experience compares to that of their competitors. This means introducing processes around how these insights are gathered, structured, and used in a holistic way to inform efficient, measurable impact. No longer is it enough to spot-optimize experience in isolated areas of the product—in order to succeed in the digital experience economy, the digital experience company must understand and improve its digital experience as a whole. The way to do this is through experience insights management (XIM)

The Value of Experience Insights Management (XIM)

The ability of a business to improve its digital experience is based on both the quality of the insights it has to make these improvements and how effectively it can mobilize and action these insights across the customer journey in a coordinated fashion and at scale. Experience insights management (XIM) brings these requirements together as the combination of processes, strategies, and technologies that enable businesses to manage the gathering, analysis, and sharing of user and customer experience insights across all digital touchpoints—a central source of truth for experience insights transformation within businesses. A robust XIM program is therefore fundamental to the success of digital experience companies of the present and future.

In previous chapters, we've already covered the *how* behind the first component of this—gathering quality insights—including the importance of a mixed-method approach to research and analytics in order to understand both the *what* and the *why* and the value of testing with real people at different sample sizes to inform different goals. This is core to the concept of XIM—robust, measurable experience insights that give businesses the confidence to inform different levels of decision-making, from tactical design iterations through to strategic competitive benchmarking. The best way to achieve this is using an XIM platform that can help automate the gathering and analysis of these insights. The second component, which will be the focus for this section, is how to then mobilize and scale these insights programmatically across the business in order to break down data silos and provide a singular view of digital experience.

The first step in addressing this is separating the signal from the noise with user and customer data and making this structured, shareable, and actionable. As Carly Fiorina, the ex-CEO of Hewlett-Packard, once said, "The goal is to turn data into information, and information into insight." Digital teams the world over face the challenge of easily locating the right data and applying it to provide insight into what they're doing. The data can reside in a computer or on a server, but to make sense of it all, they have to be able to get to the particular kinds of data they need quickly and easily. This requires the organization and classification of experience data and insights to connect them to the needs of digital teams—without having to run new research or trawl through databases in search of answers.

At UserZoom, one of the products we offer to our customers is an Experience Insights Hub (result of the acquisition of EnjoyHQ in Q1 2021) that, among many other things, delivers the following benefits:

- Stores, organizes, and classifies data from multiple sources and time periods

- Makes it easy to find and share this data for analysis and seamless, open collaboration

- Enables businesses to better understand and manage all of their experience insights and feedback by breaking down the silos between CX, UX, and/or customer support teams

- Enables businesses to do "storytelling" better and faster, to organize conclusions and present the findings directly from the product (versus having to download the data and create a PowerPoint slide deck, for instance)

An integrated Experience Insights Hub will eventually help all teams across the organization to better consolidate their efforts and collaborate efficiently and effectively, regardless of where the user insights they use originated. This collaboration is what will create the kinds of seamless digital product experiences that customers will—and to some extent, already do—demand from any brand.

The next step is to use this integrated and centralized source of truth to realize efficiencies between experience strategies in order to deliver the seamless digital experience end users expect. As companies mature, they realize that there is really no significant difference between UX (user experience) and CX (customer experience) from the end user's point of view. At the end of the day, they are only focused on the quality of their X (experience), regardless of which department or strategy was employed to produce it. The way things are headed, there won't be the separation of these roles we have today; users will be users, whether they're prospects, customers, or employees. This is where leadership must take the initiative to drive digital experience transformation, partnering with third-party experts and internal stakeholders across design, product, marketing, support, engineering, and ops to bring digital experience under one roof and place it in the center of their strategy.

At the end of the day, a DX company must be, above all, *a truly customer-centric organization*, because it knows all about its customers' needs, attitudes, and behaviors and enables them to do things the way they want to, when they want to, easily and conveniently: buy products, return products, sign up for subscriptions, cancel subscriptions, download games, movies, and podcasts, etc. Consumers have more choices than ever before, and they *will* choose companies that provide them with the best user interface and the best customer experience. And even if you want to help them interact with your company, you won't be able to, because they *want* to do it on their own, they are getting used to doing it on their own, and they're also not standing in front of you to be helped. Your "help" *has to be* incorporated into your website or app—and the only way you can provide that intelligently is if you really know how users are experiencing your website or app through quality insights that extend beyond departmental boundaries to give a 360-degree view of your digital experience.

─────────────── **KEY TAKEAWAYS** ───────────────

▶ The challenge is bringing together all your user experience data, winnowing it, organizing it, classifying it, sharing it, and making it searchable—so it's not overwhelming and can be accessed by anybody who needs it.

▶ What you need to process all of this data effectively is an experience insights management (XIM) program.

► An XIM platform is an experience research and insights ecosystem that

▷ enables the gathering and analysis of robust experience insights that allow digital teams to understand, measure, and make decisions on their digital experience;

▷ stores, organizes, and classifies data from multiple sources and time periods;

▷ makes it easy to find and share this data for analysis and seamless, open collaboration; and

▷ enables businesses to better understand and manage all of their experience insights by breaking down the silos between CX and UX teams and strategies,

► The collaboration made possible by XIM programs and systems is what will create the kinds of seamless digital experiences that customers will—and to some extent, already do—demand from a product, brand, or company.

Staying Ahead of the Competition to Realize Your Dream

If you're a competitive person, that stays with you. You don't stop. You always look over your shoulder.
—EARVIN "MAGIC" JOHNSON

The second time I met Magic Johnson was at the Qualtrics X4 Experience Management Summit in 2019. He was a speaker at the conference, and I was determined to take advantage of that opportunity to reconnect with him. But how? I was one of eight thousand conference participants, many of whom would want to meet Magic. It wasn't as if I worked for Qualtrics or had some kind of "in" with the conference organizers. So I tweeted about his appearance at the conference twenty-four hours before his speech, saying it would be a dream come true to meet him.

The next morning, I got an email from the Qualtrics event marketing team telling me to be in a certain spot at the conference venue at a time that was exactly five minutes before the end of Magic's speech.

When I arrived, there were about twenty-five of us who had been given this opportunity, all waiting to meet him. Each one of us got to meet the "magic man" individually and spend a couple of minutes with him and have a picture taken. When it was my turn, I said, "You won't believe this—and you won't recognize me, of course—but we met thirty years ago at the Forum, after a game, when I was a high school basketball player."

And he said, "Wow. Thirty years ago? Really? No way!" And I told him the story about being a foreign exchange student and him being my hero and my coach bringing me to meet him. And his eyes got big, and he got that big smile on his face—just like the first time—and he actually gave me a hug. It was just phenomenal.

So, my dream came true—a second time. And it's also come true with building a successful company like UserZoom. Maybe that's why I believe that if you dream big and really go after it, your dreams really can come true.

There is a lot of competition out there among digital experience companies—which, as the title of this book says, are really all companies in the digital age—and it's a tough thing to stay ahead of the competition. But if you do things right, if you get the help you need to provide the best UX, users will flock to your website or your app, and you can achieve great success much more quickly than ever before. And if you keep on top of your UX, continually testing and improving it, you'll stay ahead of the competition, and your success can last a long, long time.

I hope your dreams for your company come true and that this book will assist you—the way Magic Johnson always assisted his teammates—to achieve that ambitious goal.